The
Mystic Hare
Four Seasons
Design and Colouring
Book

Emma Palmer

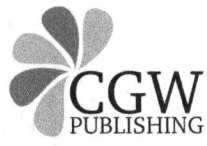

CGW
PUBLISHING

2017

The Mystic Hare Four Seasons Design and Colouring Book

First Edition: October 2017

ISBN 978-1-908293-44-2

Published by:

CGW Publishing
B 1502
PO Box 15113
Birmingham
B2 2NJ
United Kingdom

www.cgwpublishing.com

mail@cgwpublishing.com

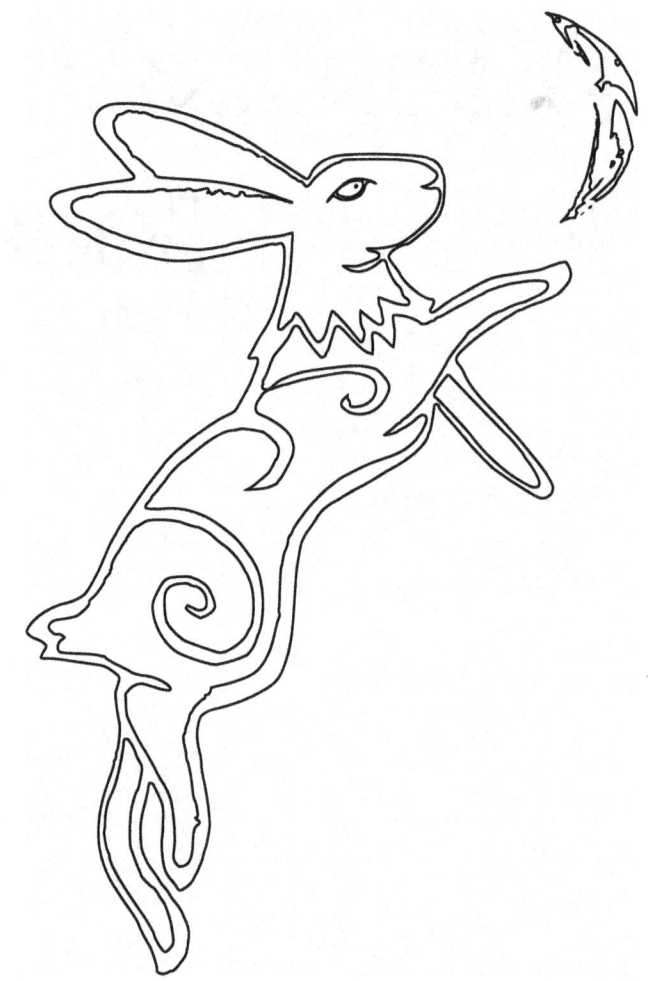

The Mystic Hare Four Seasons Design and Colouring Book

Spring

Dancing Hares

Loving Lovebirds

Proud Rooster

Emerging Butterfly

Easter Eggs

Sociable Bees

Pisces the Fish

Aries the Ram

Taurus the Bull

Summer

Floating Dragonfly

Strong Elephant

Wise Turtle

Sparkling Starfish

Cheeky Giraffes

Stretching Butterfly

Gemini the Twins

Cancer the Crab

Leo the Lion

Autumn

Night Owl

Halloween Cat

Pumpkin Mice

Nutty Squirrel

Changing Chameleon

Clever Owl

Virgo the Innocent

Libra the Balance

Scorpio the Scorpion

Winter

Regal Stag

Curious Robin

Thoughtful Hare

Arctic Fox

Kissing Hares

Highland Cow

Sagittarius the Archer

Capricorn the Goat

Aquarius the Water Bearer

Welcome to my Four Seasons Design and Colouring Book. As you can see, I have arranged the book into the four seasons with designs featuring both seasonal animals as well as images representing the zodiac signs for each season.

This is more than just a colouring book however; some of the designs are deliberately left open for you to add your own design elements. You'll be able to develop your own creativity as well as your colouring skill as you enjoy completing the designs. There are even some blank pages at the end of the book for you to practice on. I find designing and colouring a very soothing thing to do and a real stress buster, and it's so much nicer to develop your creativity rather than just to watch TV.

Here are some ideas for design elements that you might think about incorporating, and you might also look around you for inspiration, perhaps in fabrics, clothing, product packaging and of course the patterns that you'll find in nature such as waves, clouds, leaves, pine cones and so on.

All of my work is hand drawn, and now it's time for you to become part of the creative process as you turn these outlines into your own unique works of art.

My hope is that you'll experience much more than the satisfaction of adding colour to the images, you will also feel the pleasure of steering your own designs. I would always encourage you to embellish and add design elements to each page even if they are outside the image. So let yourself go and think outside the box!

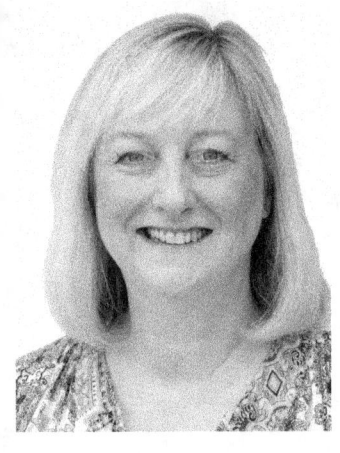

I originally trained as a textile designer in the 1980s at Dewsbury & Batley Art College, West Yorkshire and more recently I have turned to other media including canvasses, prints, glassware, ceramics, stained glass and fabrics. The creative process can't be constrained to one medium and I encourage you to try out your design ideas in different ways too.

My work is highly illustrative and much of it is more design-led as opposed to 'fine art', featuring a combination of natural themes as well as more abstract or geometric patterns. I feel that these concepts connect me back to my artistic roots in textile design, and draw on many of the themes that I personally enjoy exploring.

Many of my designs are spiritual in nature as I have been inspired by the tarot and astrology, and you might also like to explore the symbolism of the designs in this book as you enjoy adding your own colours and themes. You use symbols every day; language, icons, road signs, even brand logos, and the symbols that you are drawn to say something about you, so do explore them as you add your own individuality to these pages, and as you do that, you will discover your own unique style as I have discovered mine. You might recognise that style running through these pages, as well as different ideas that I continually incorporate as my work evolves.

Whether you're enjoying this book to develop your creativity or just to relax your mind, you can find a connection with the images and the natural world that they represent and perhaps discover more about yourself in the process. Have fun!

You can find out more about my work at my website:

www.mystichare.com

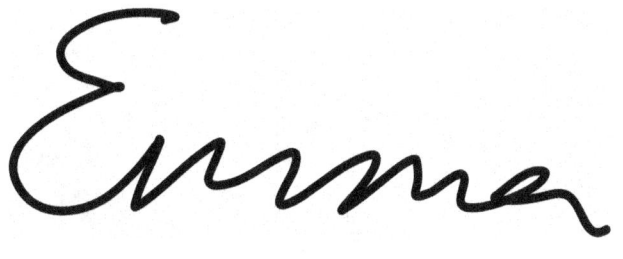

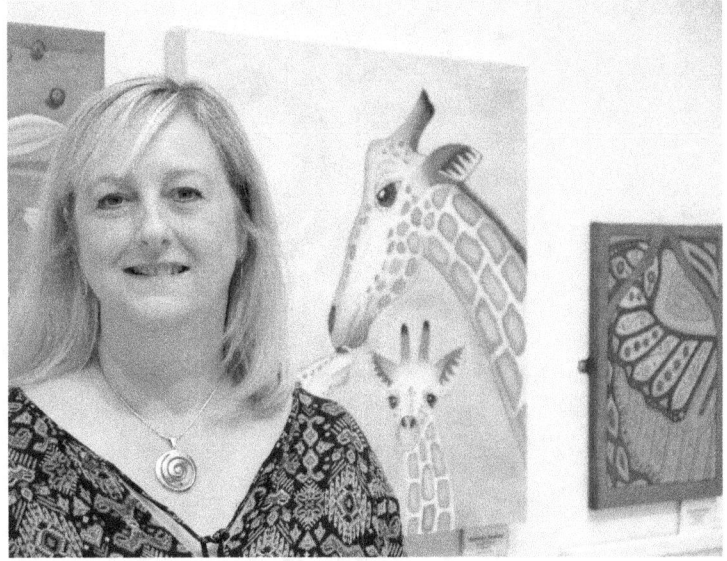

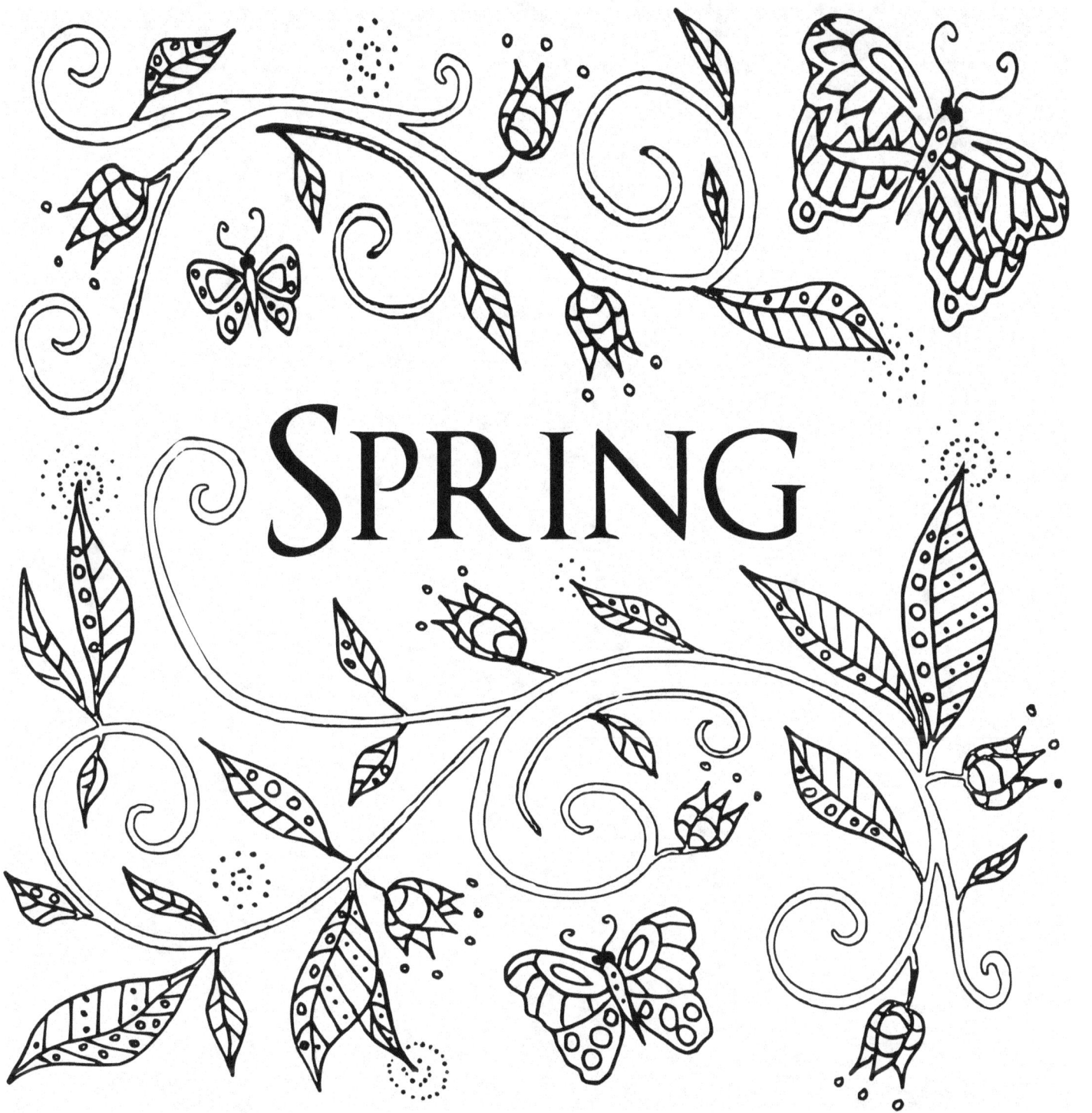

SPRING

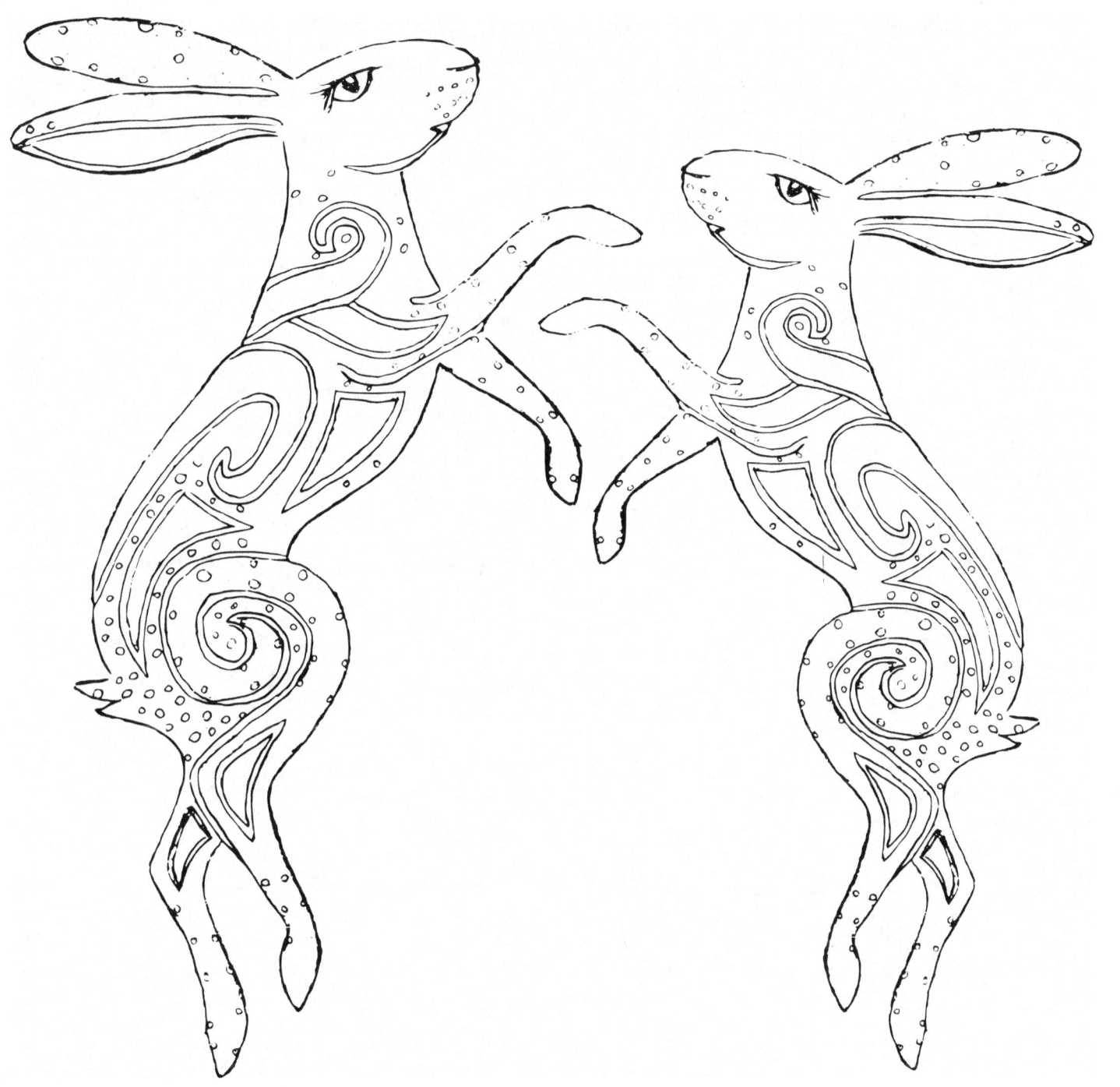

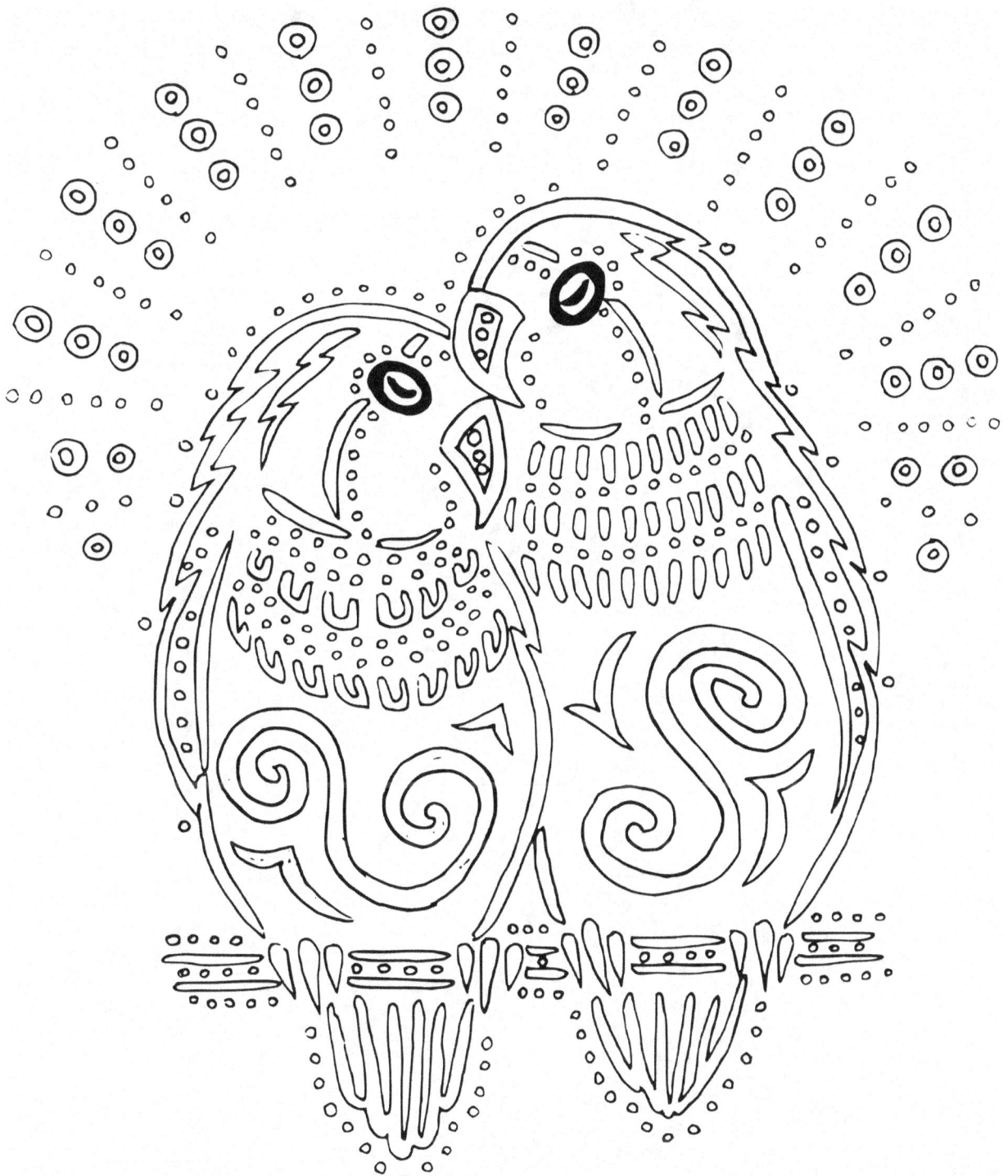

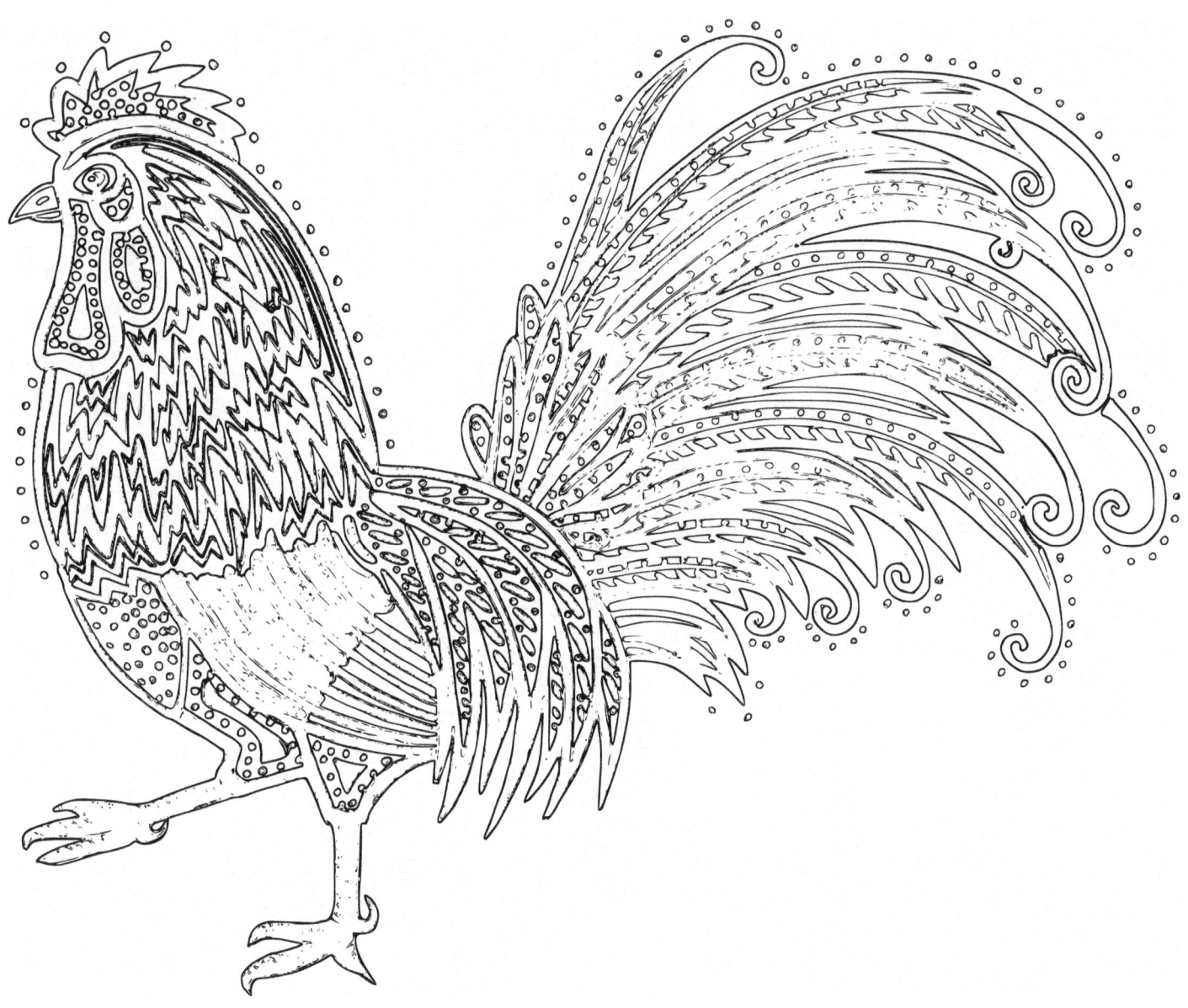

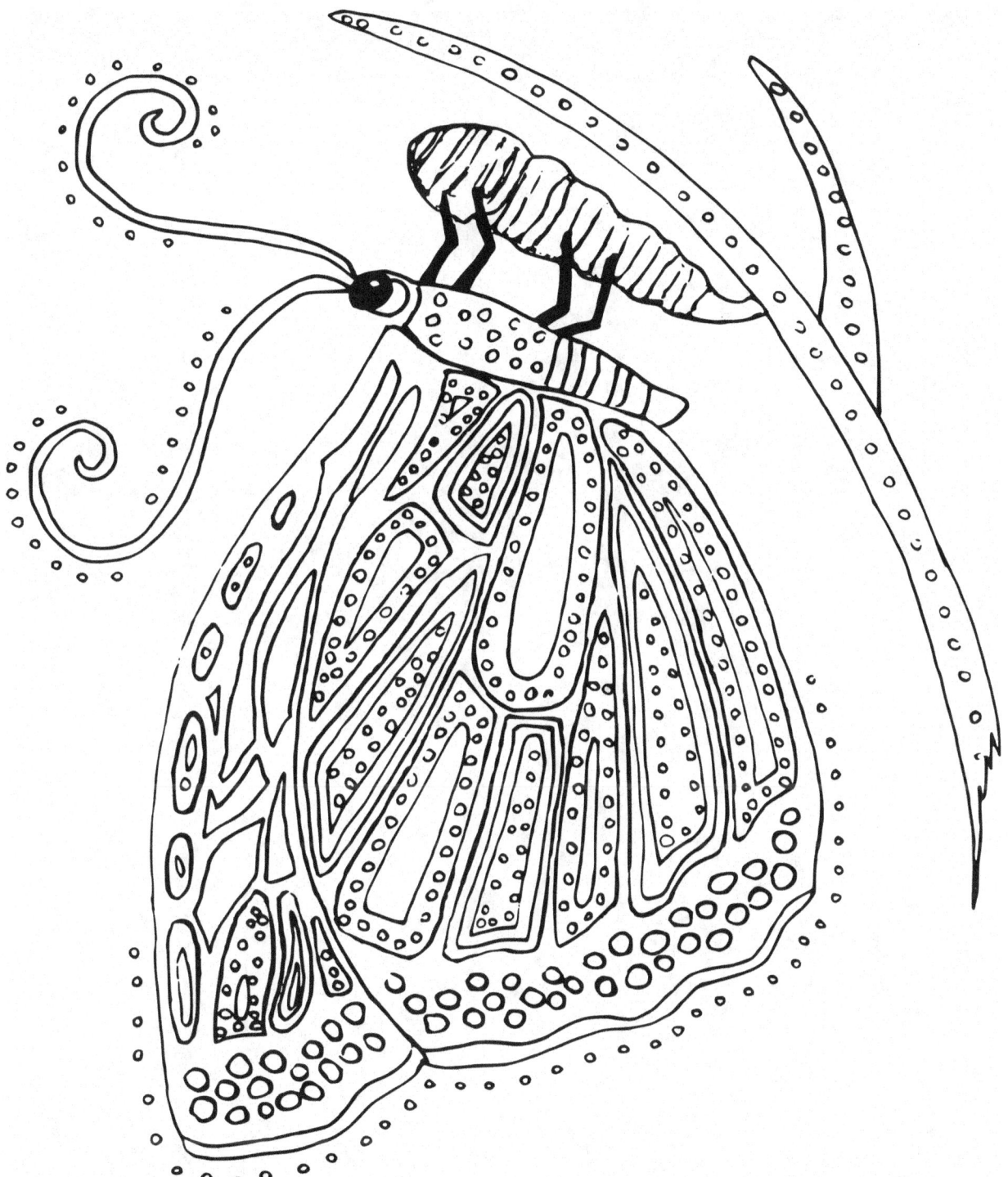

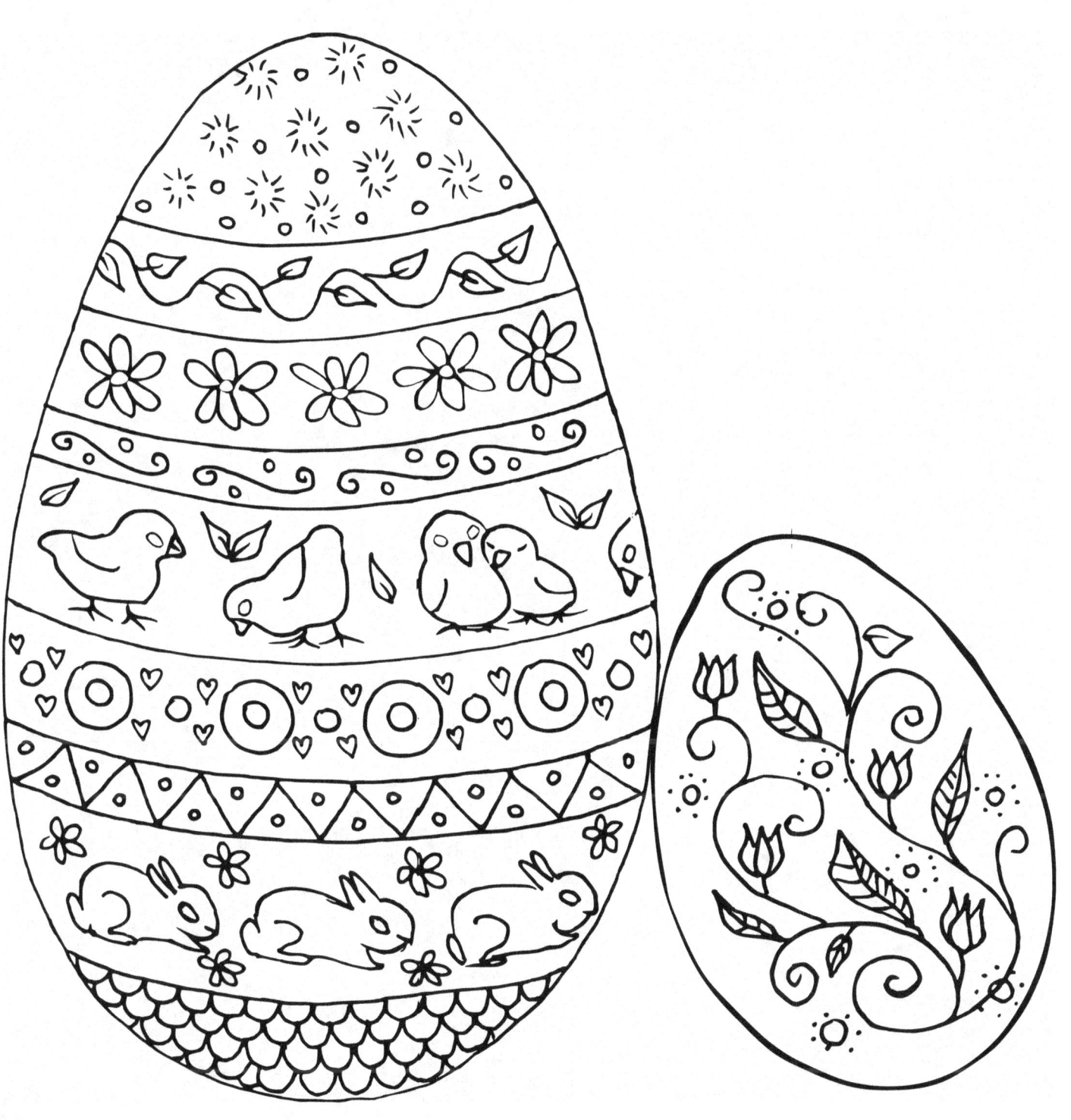

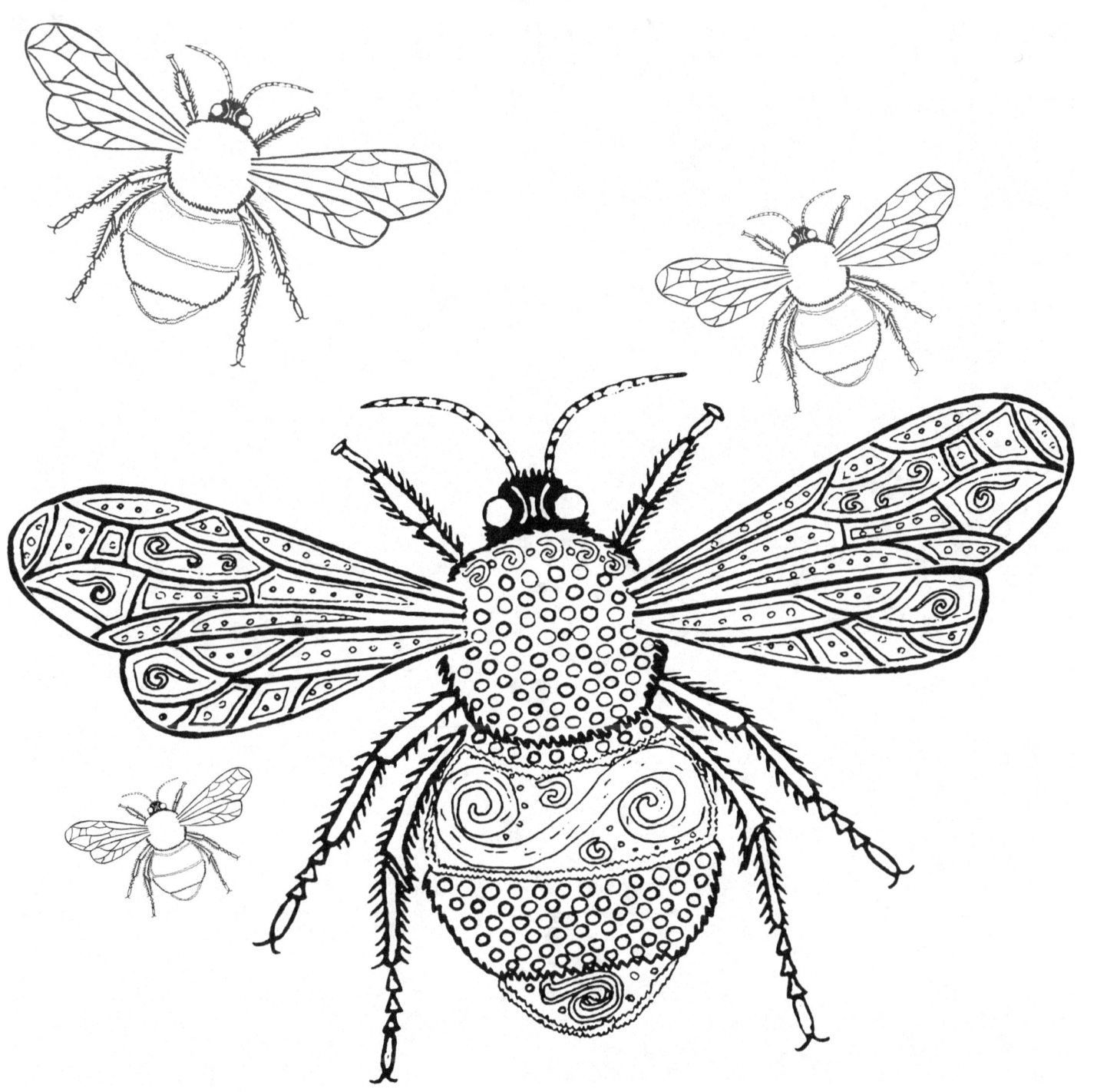

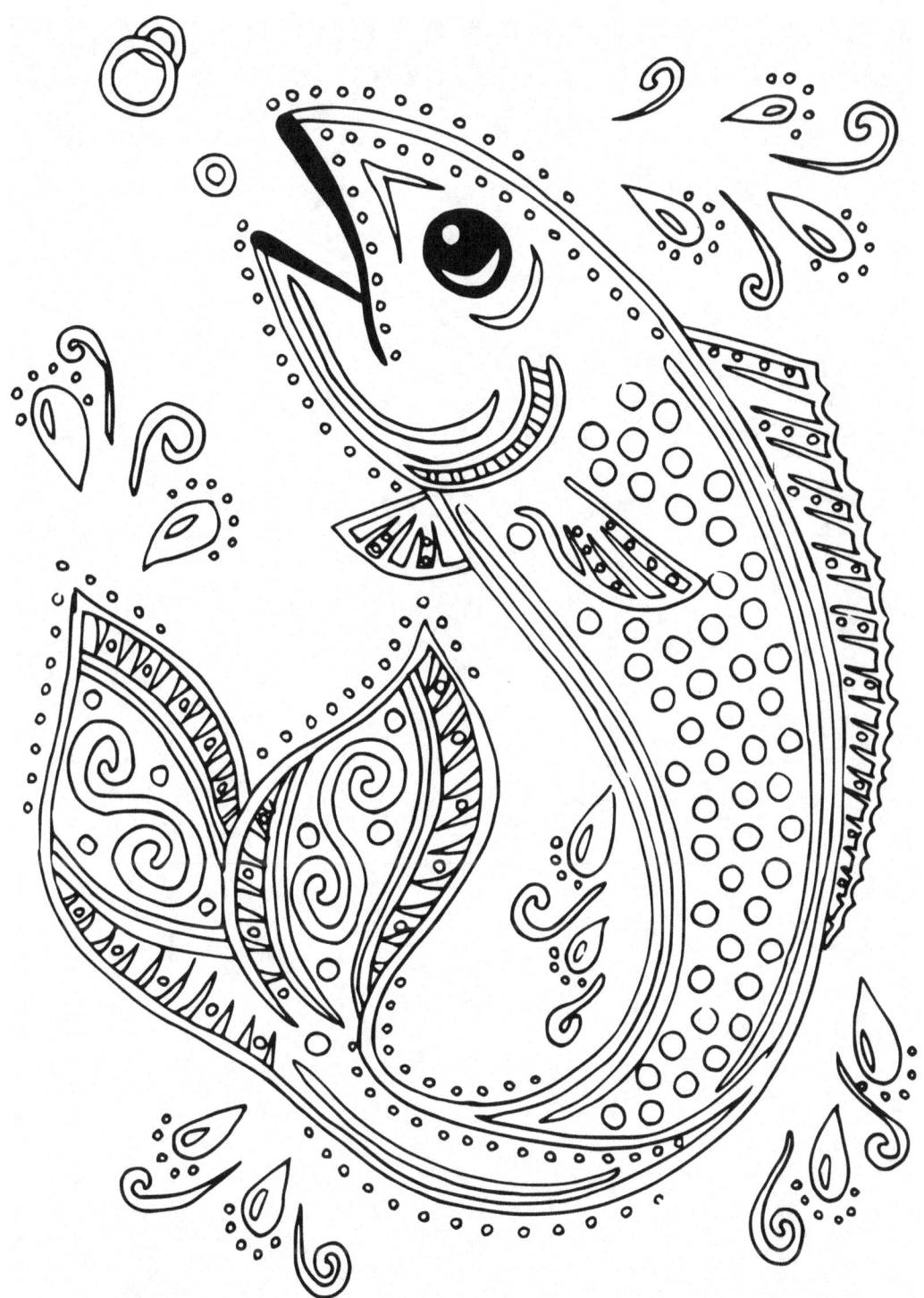

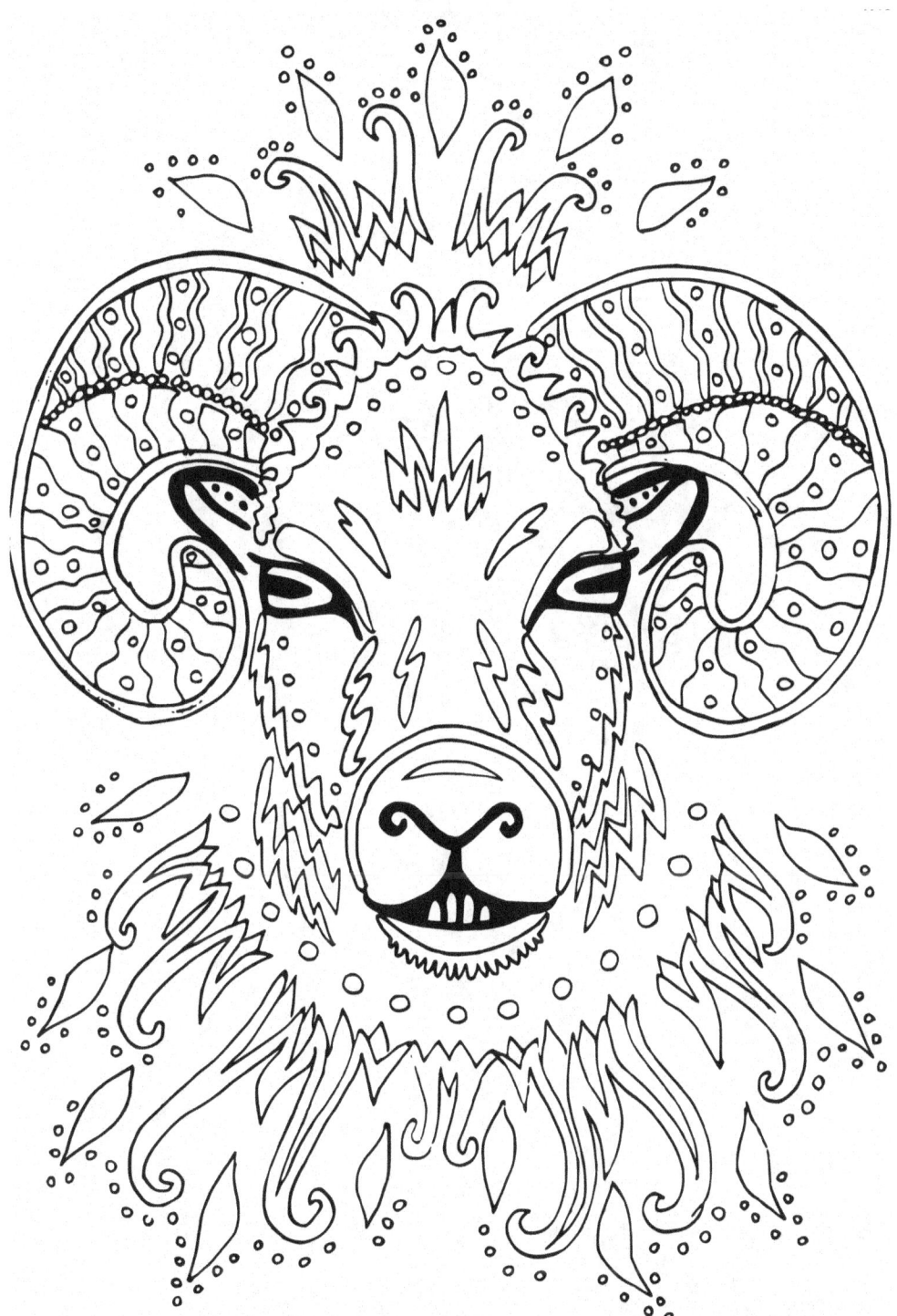

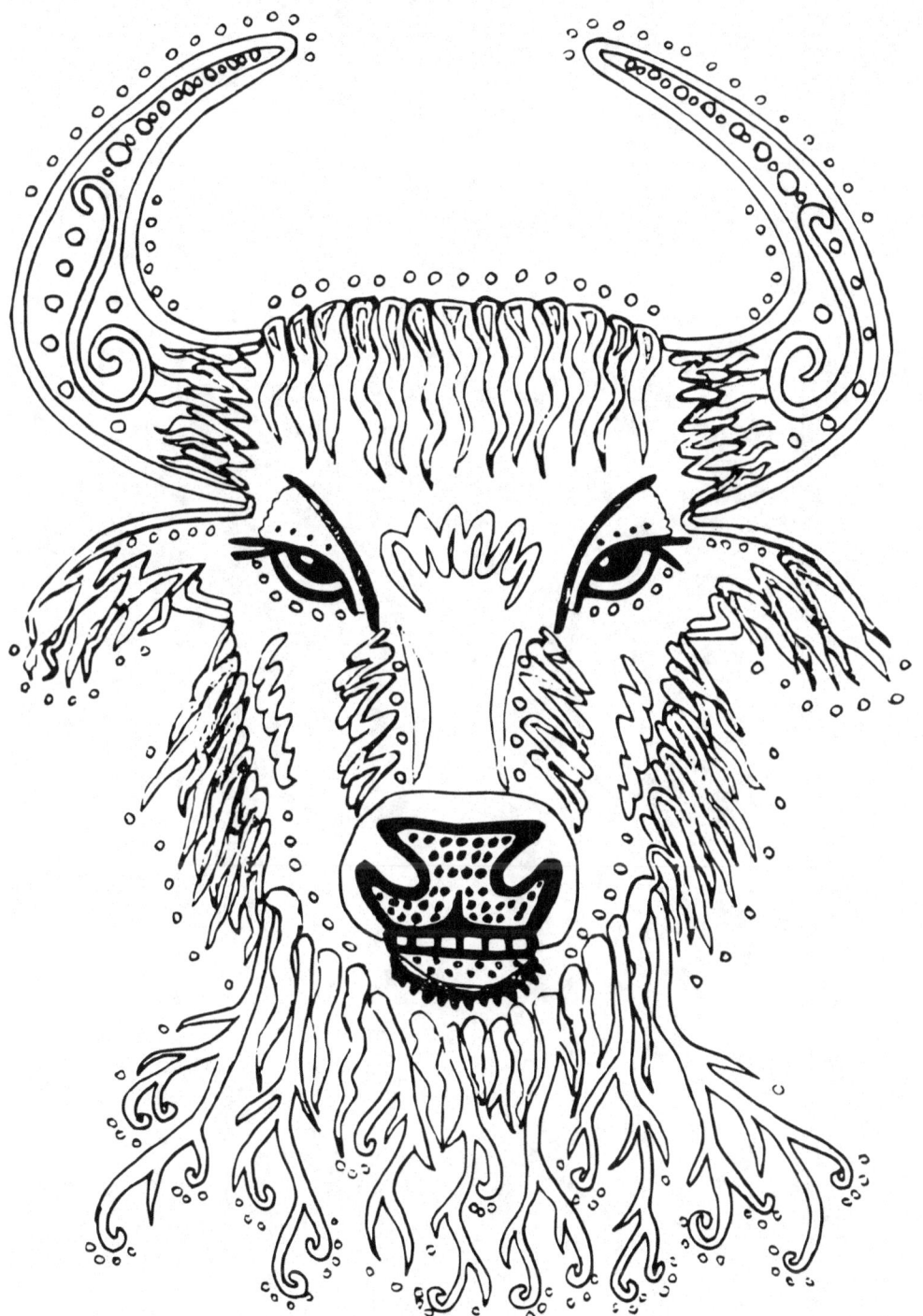

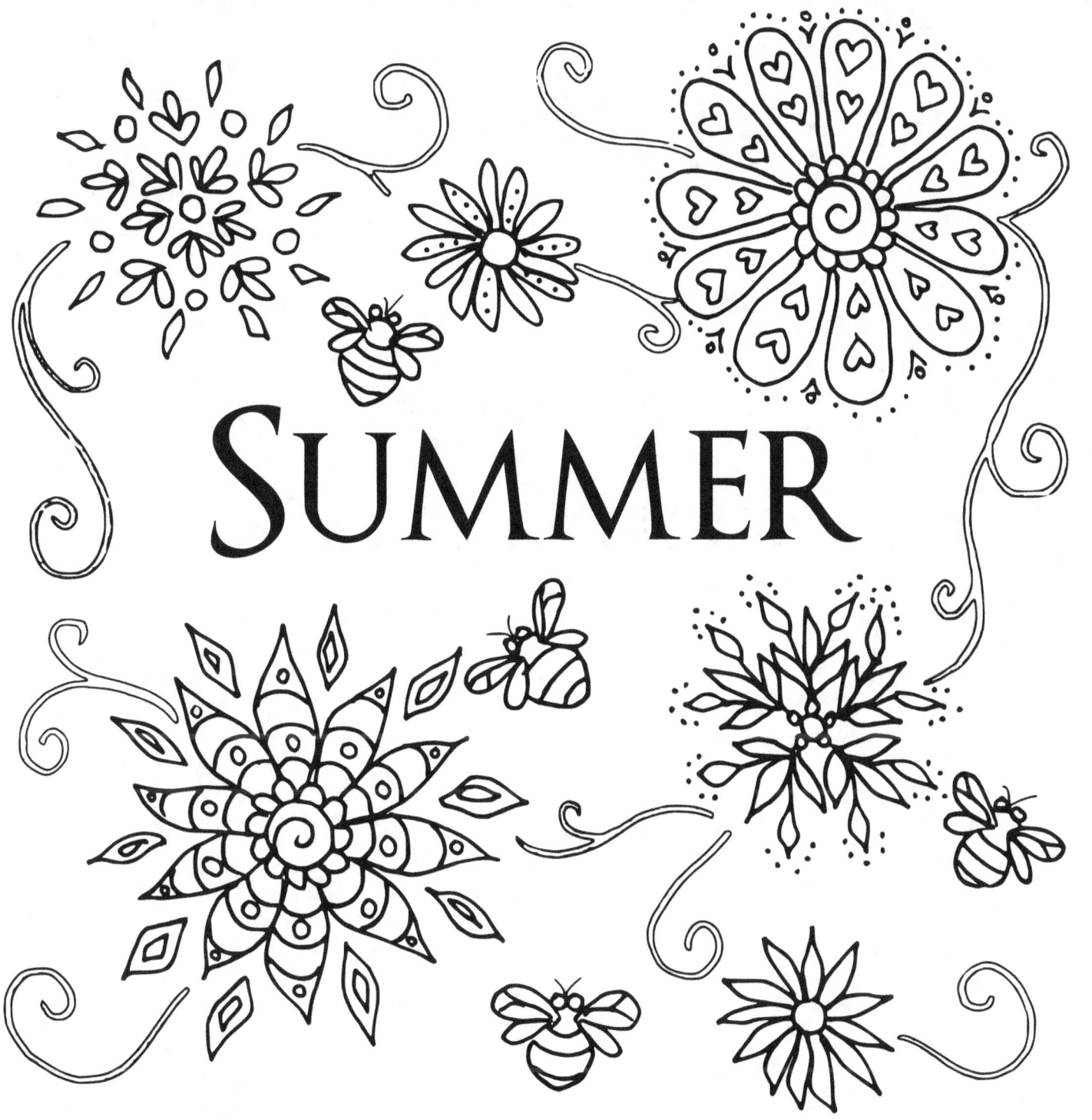

SUMMER

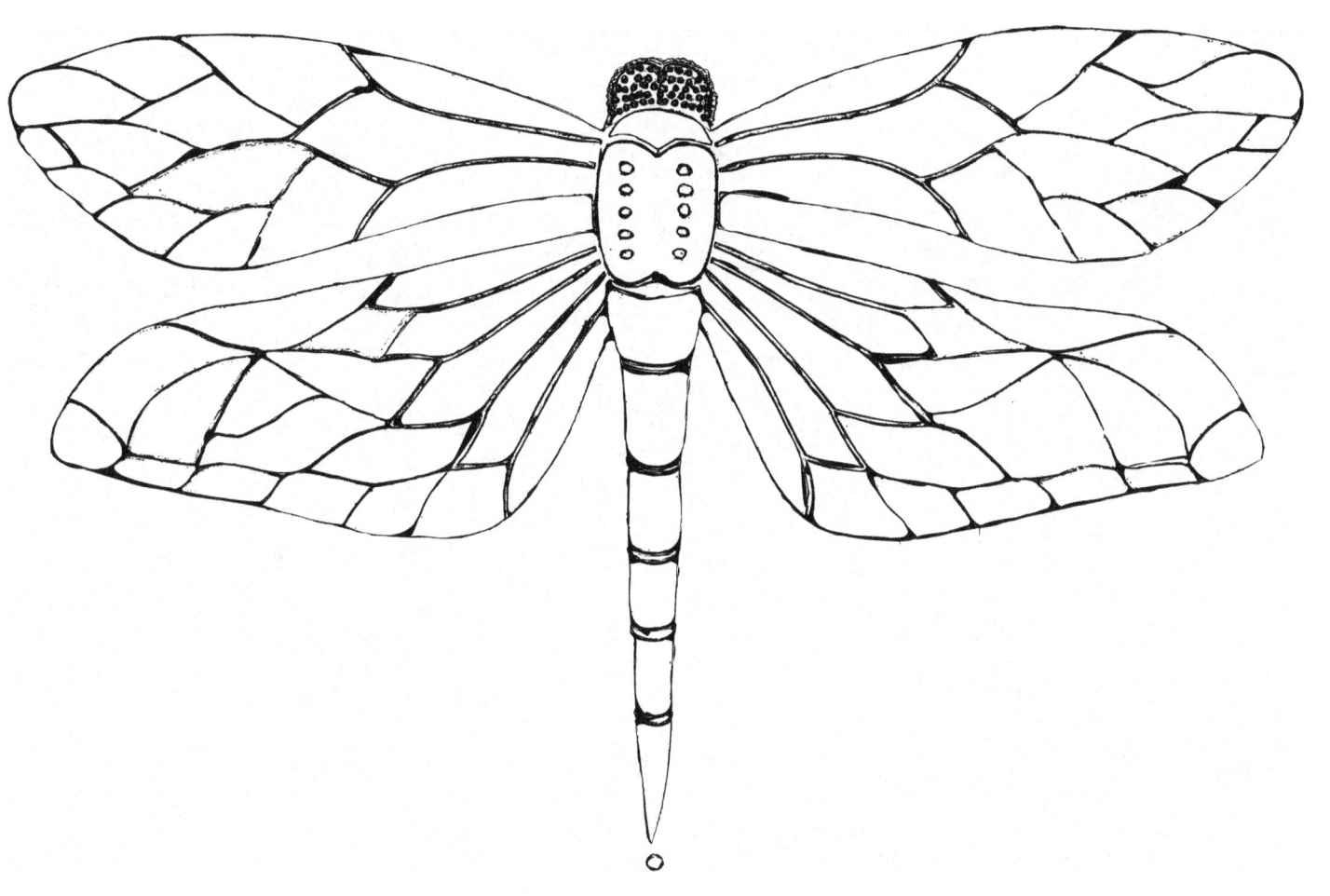

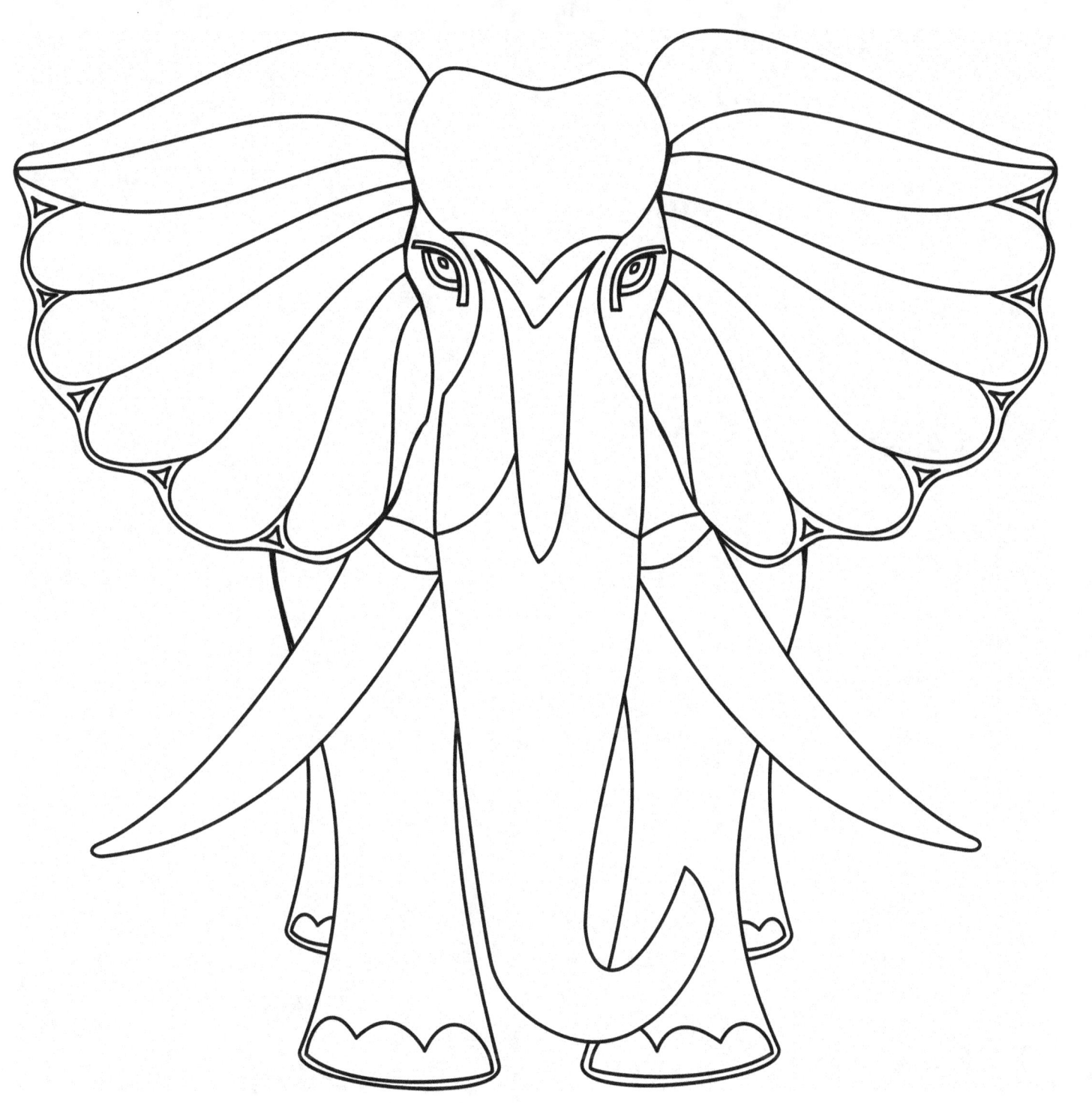

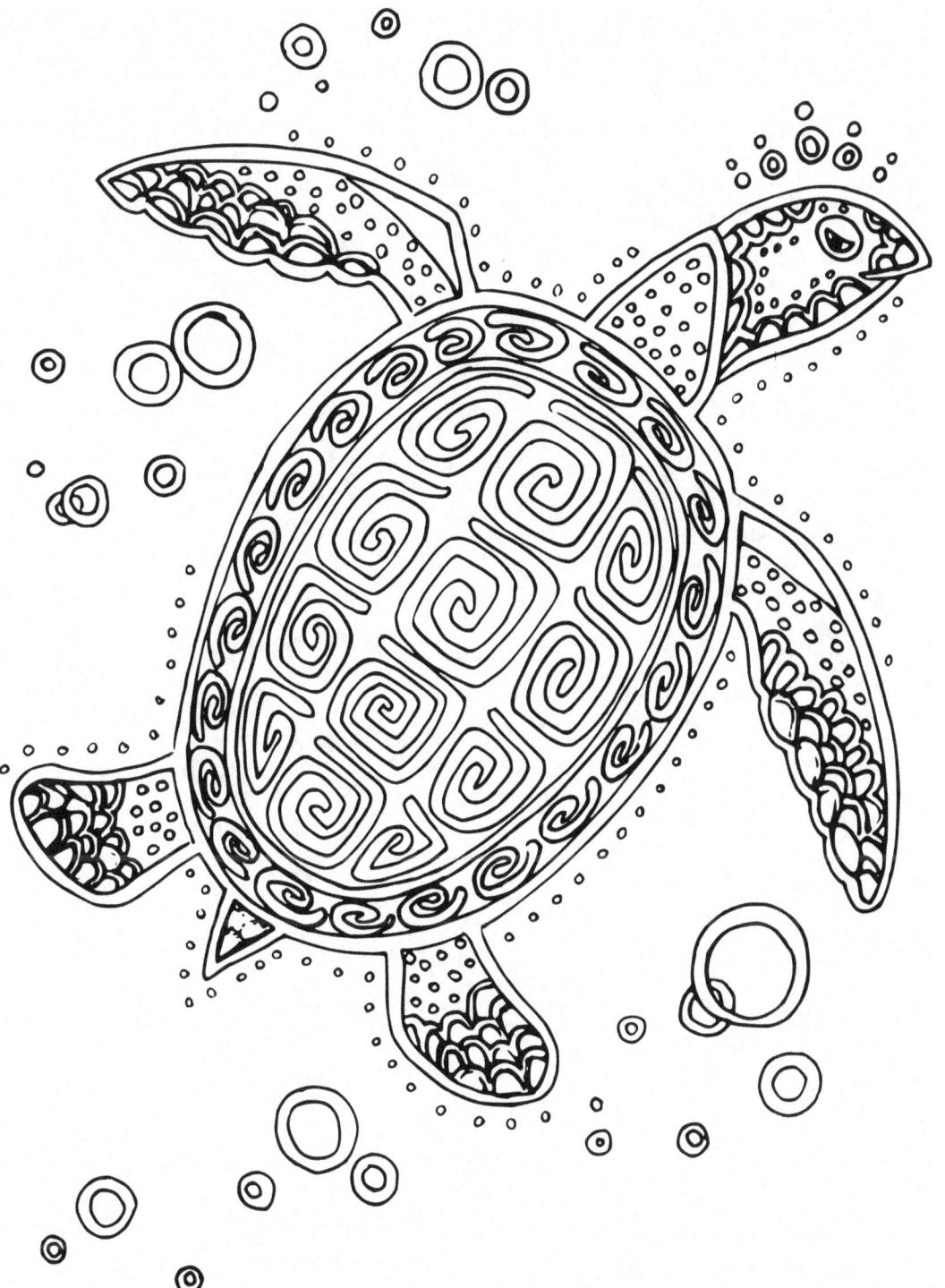

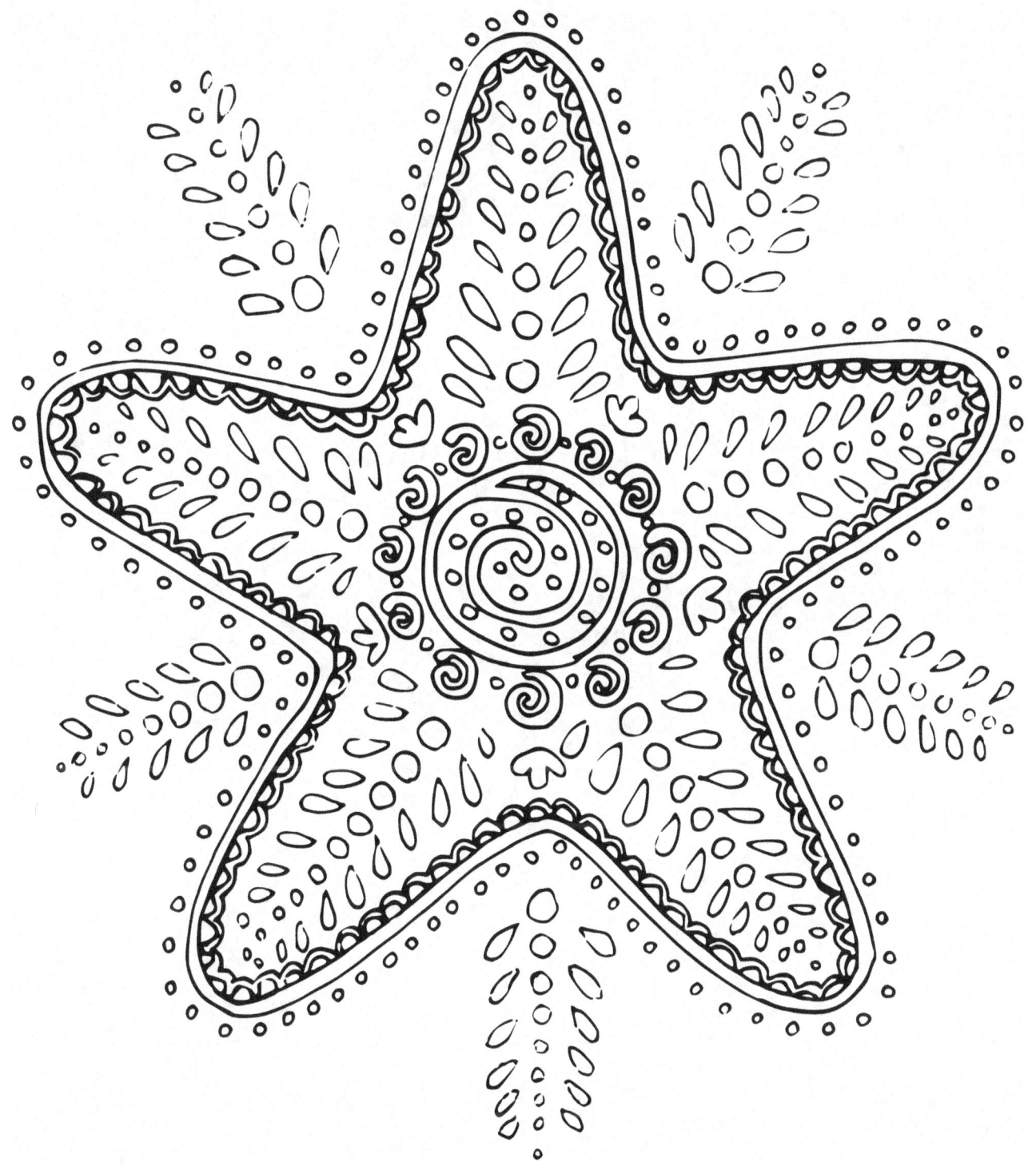

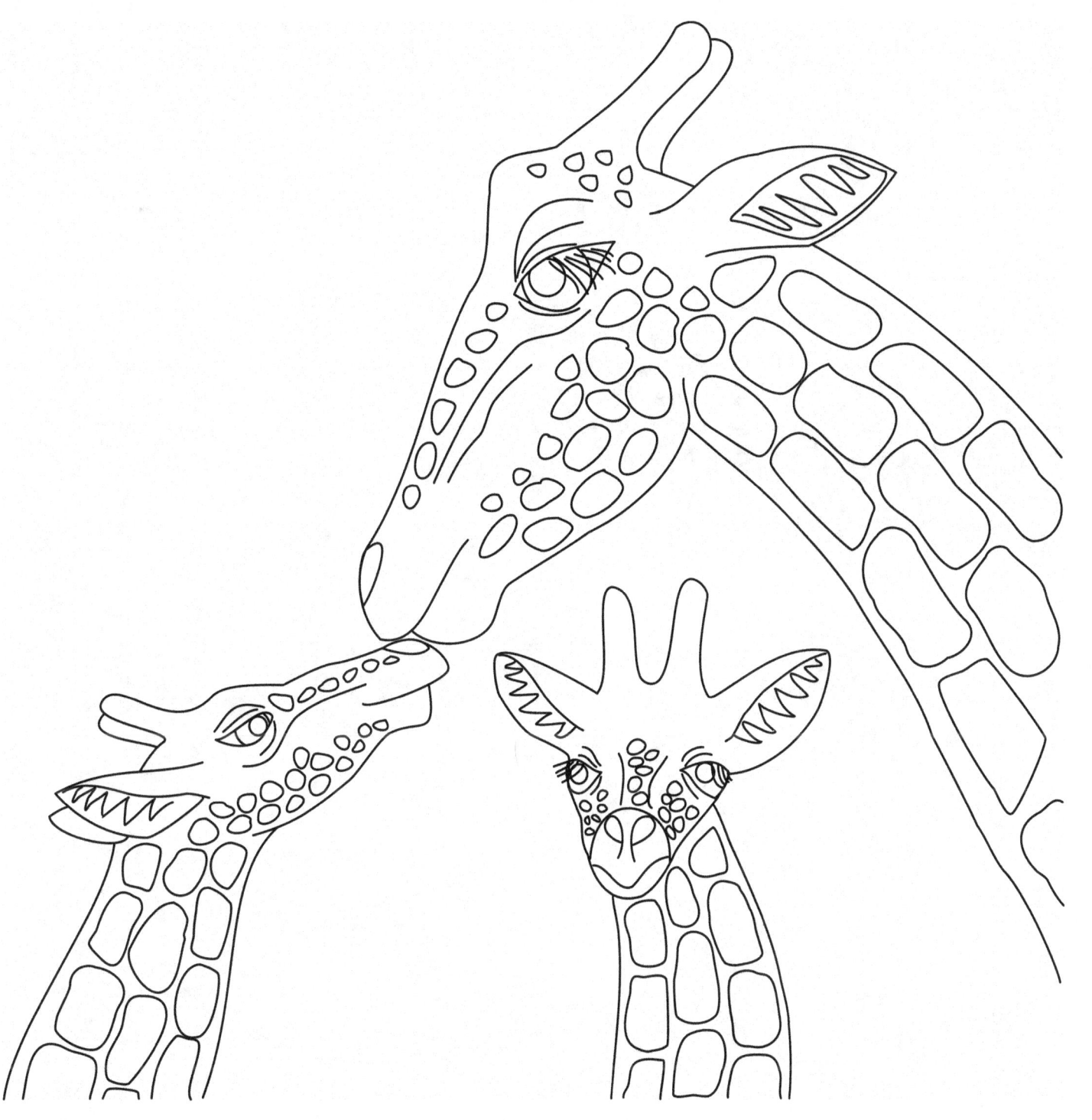

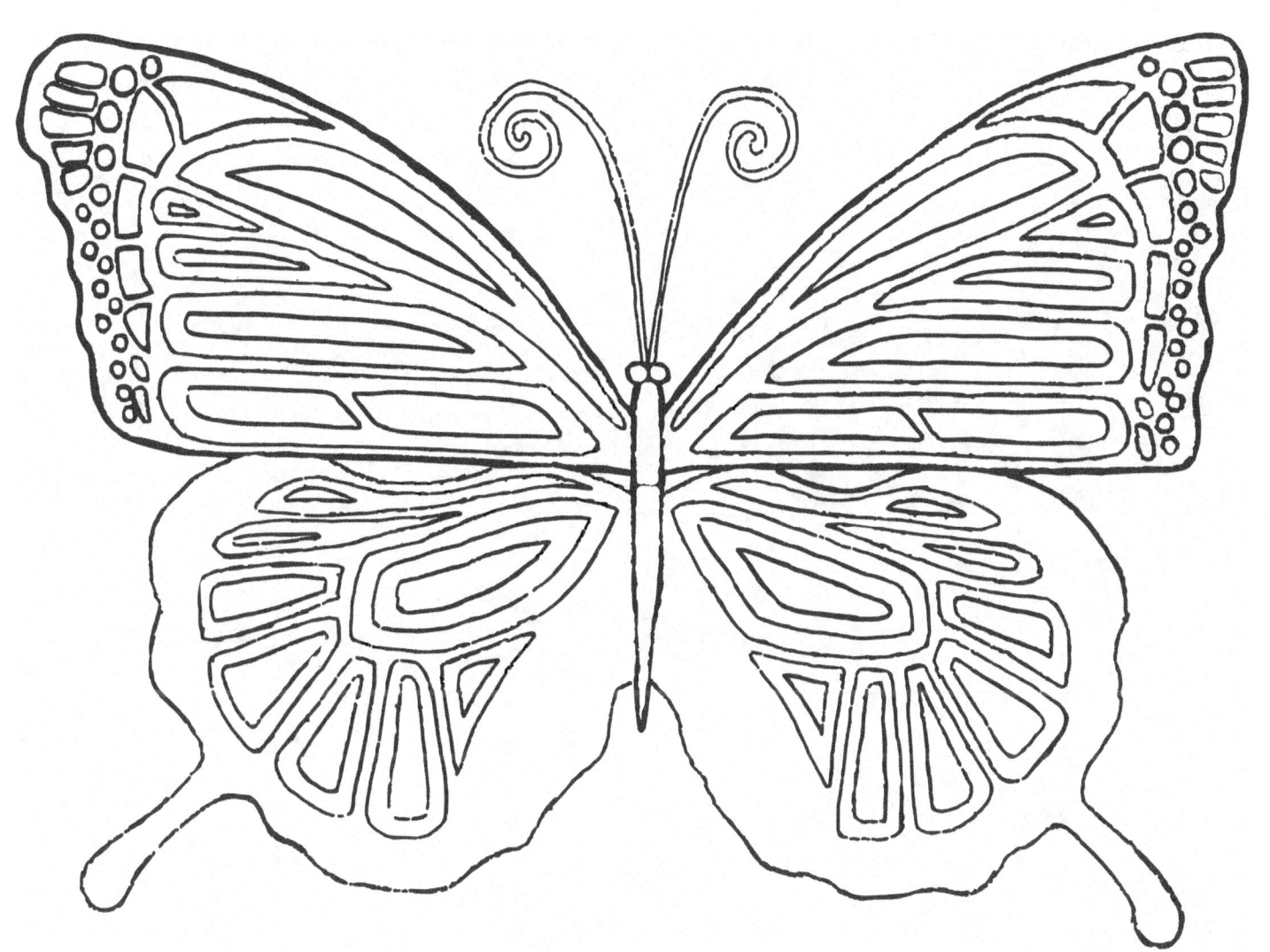

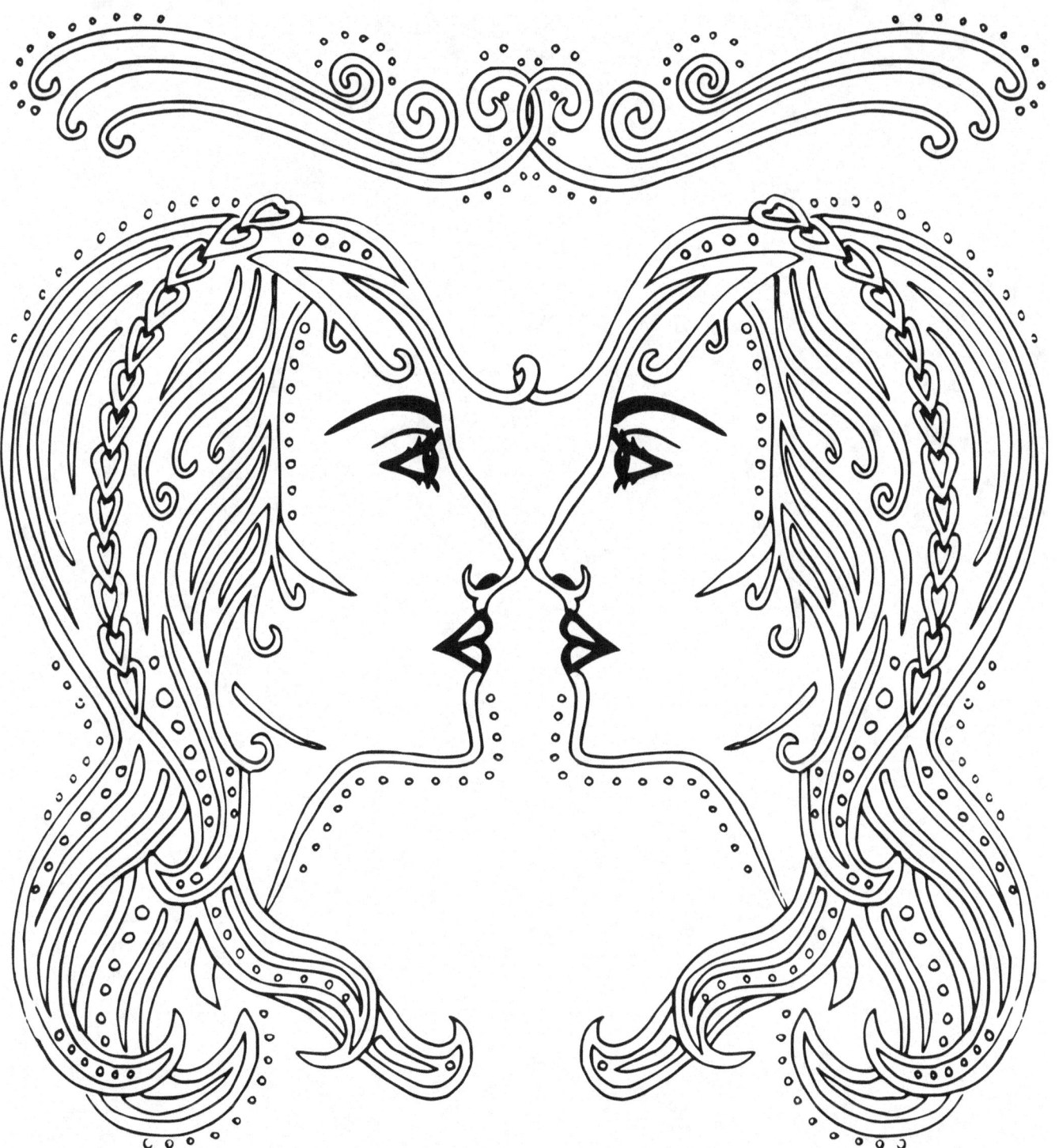

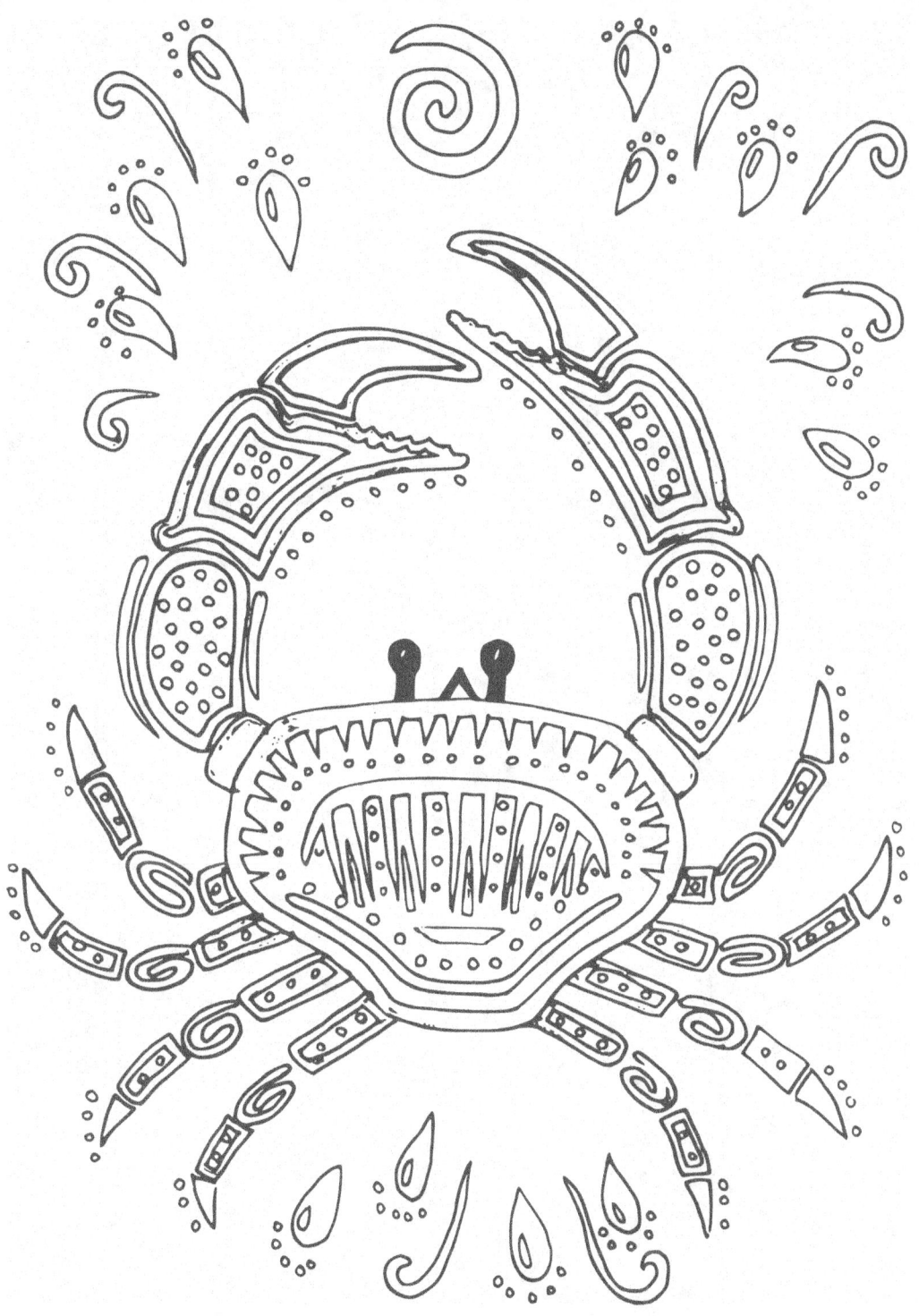

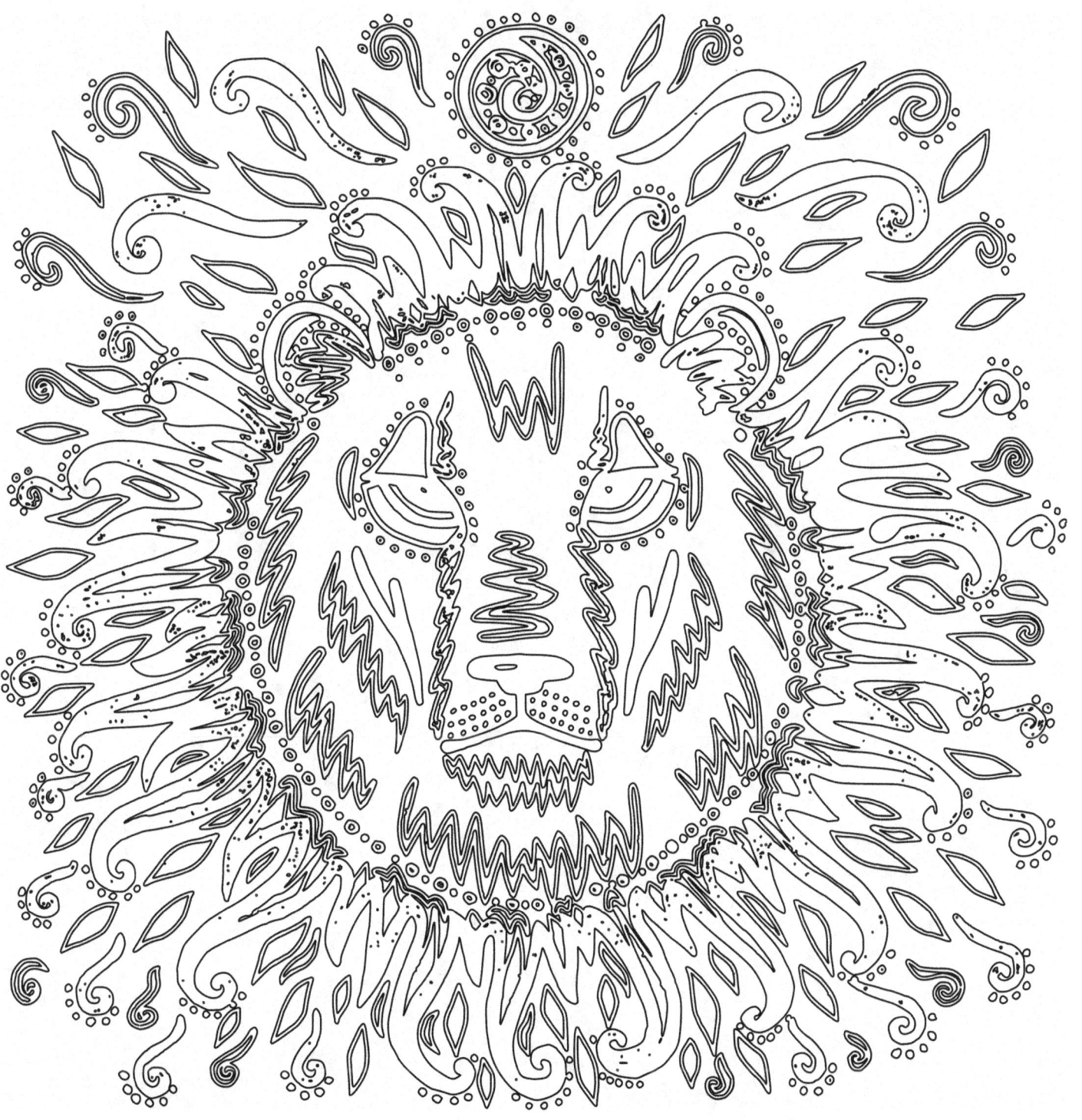

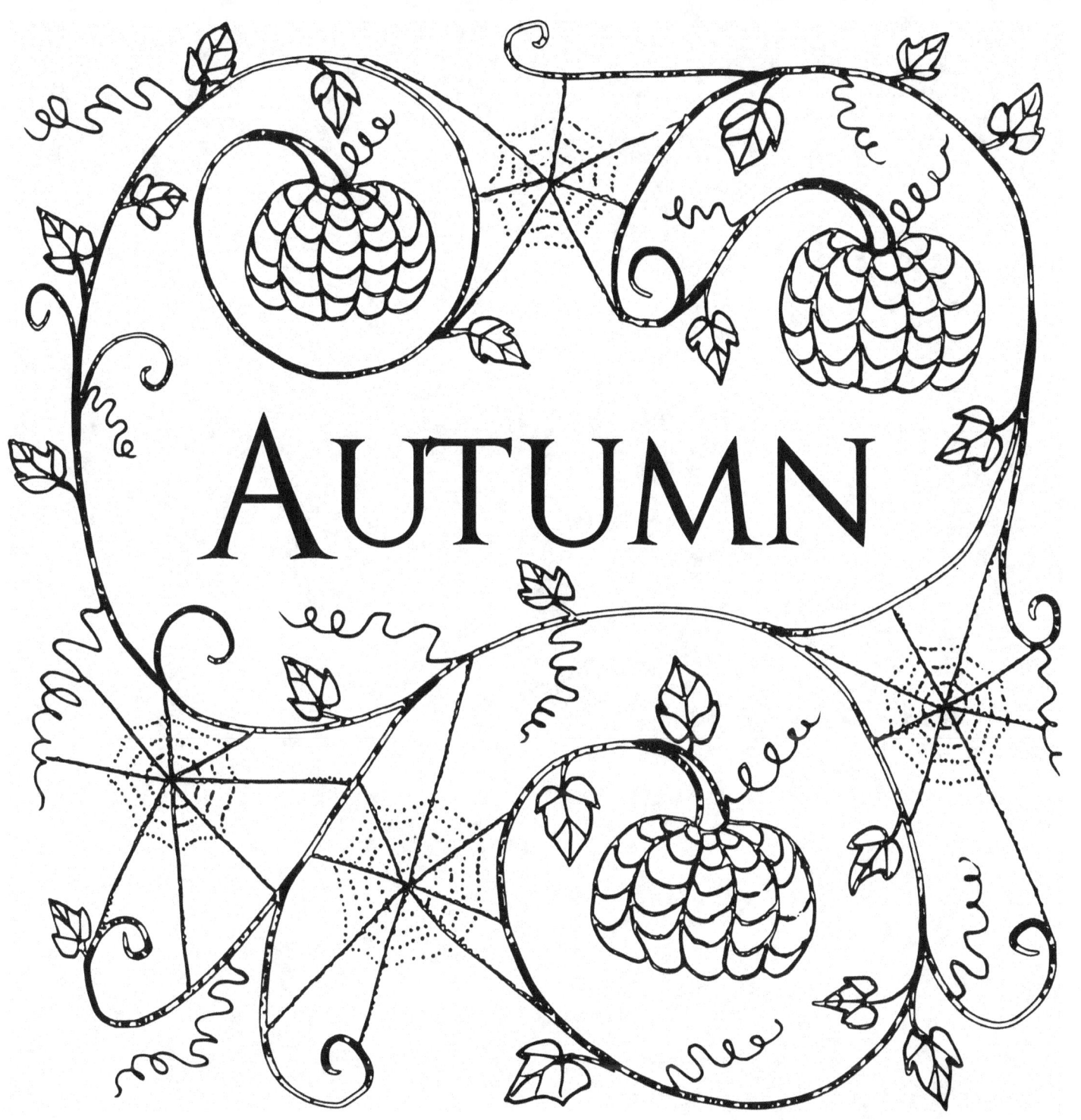

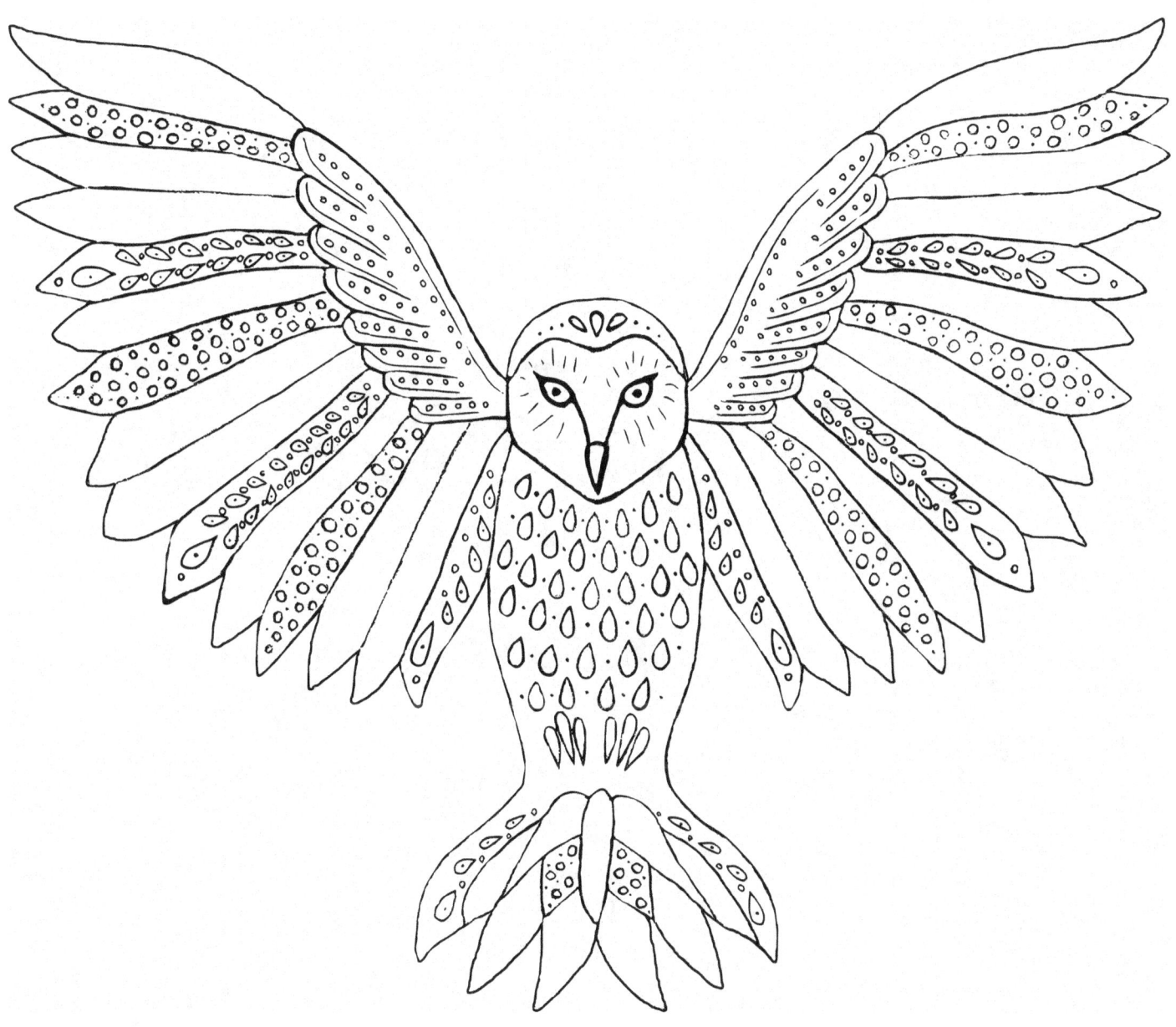

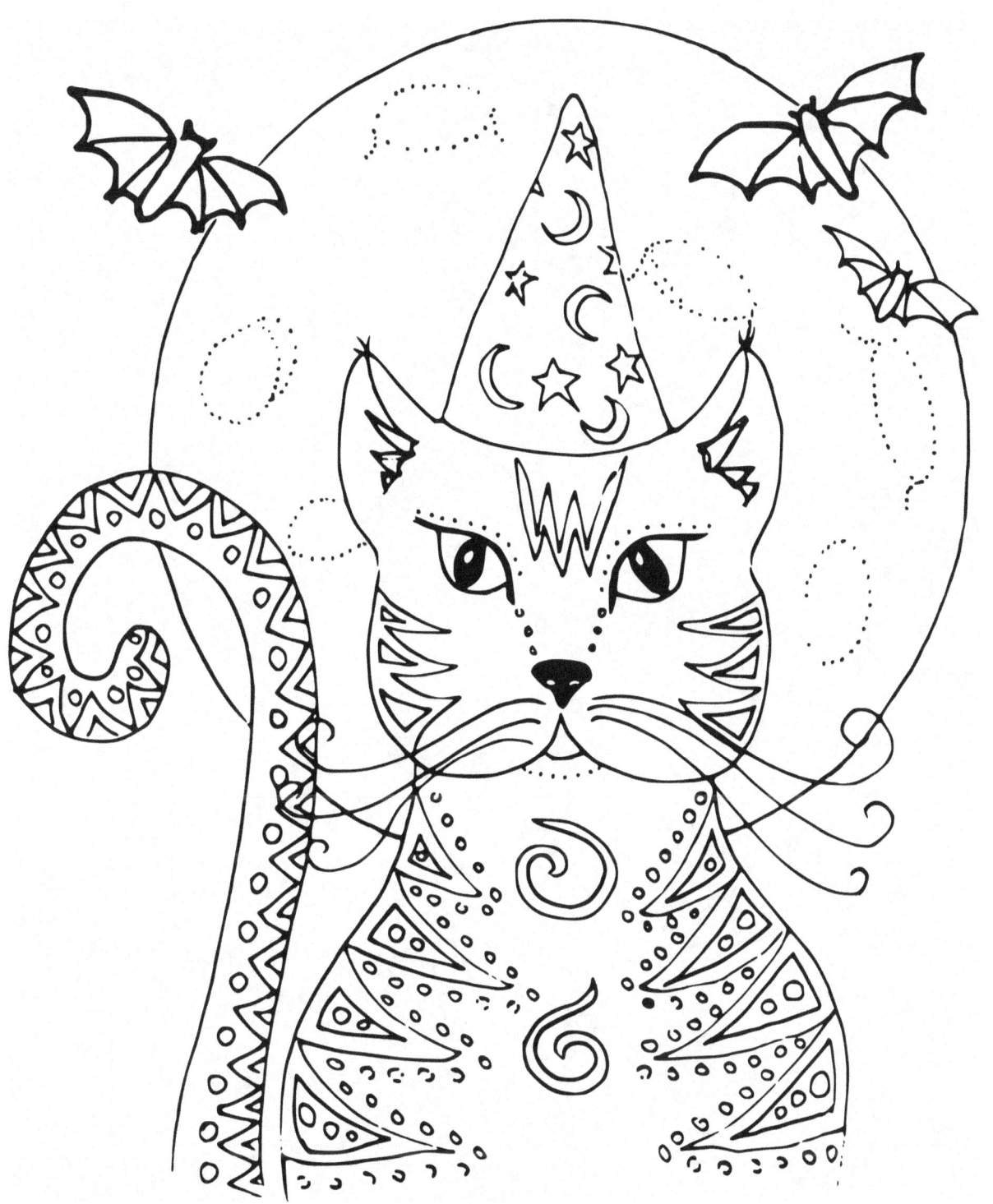

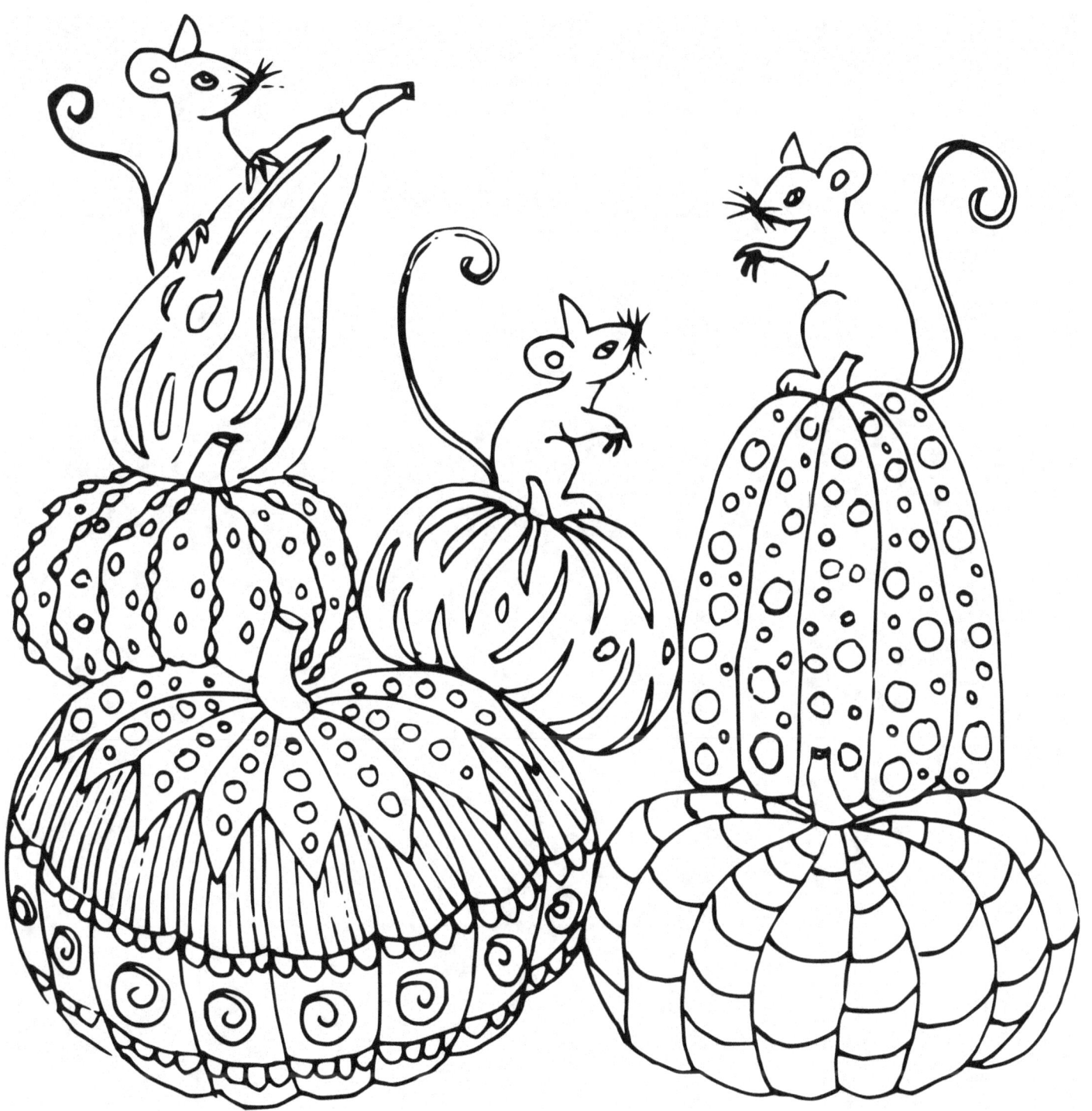

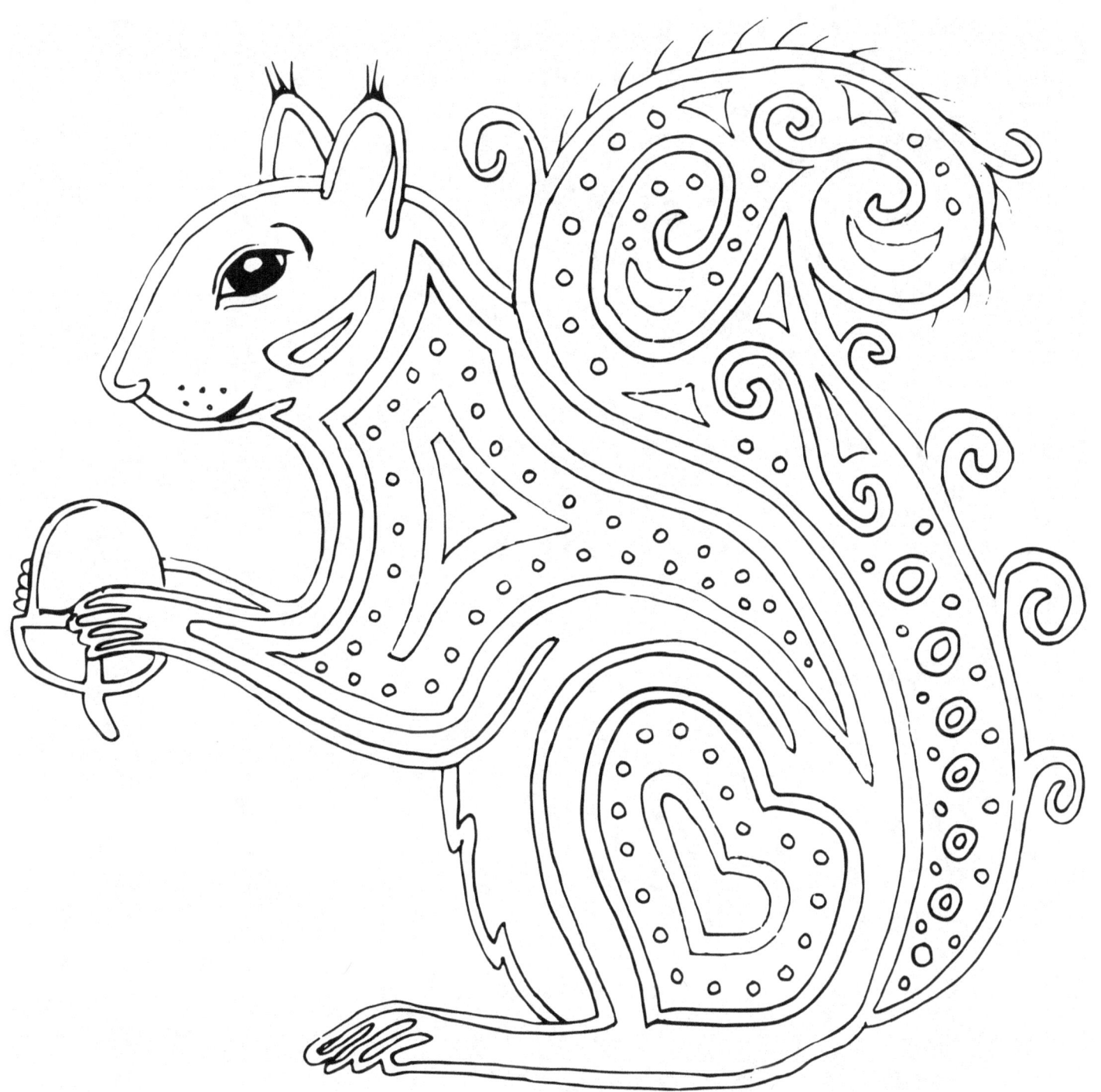

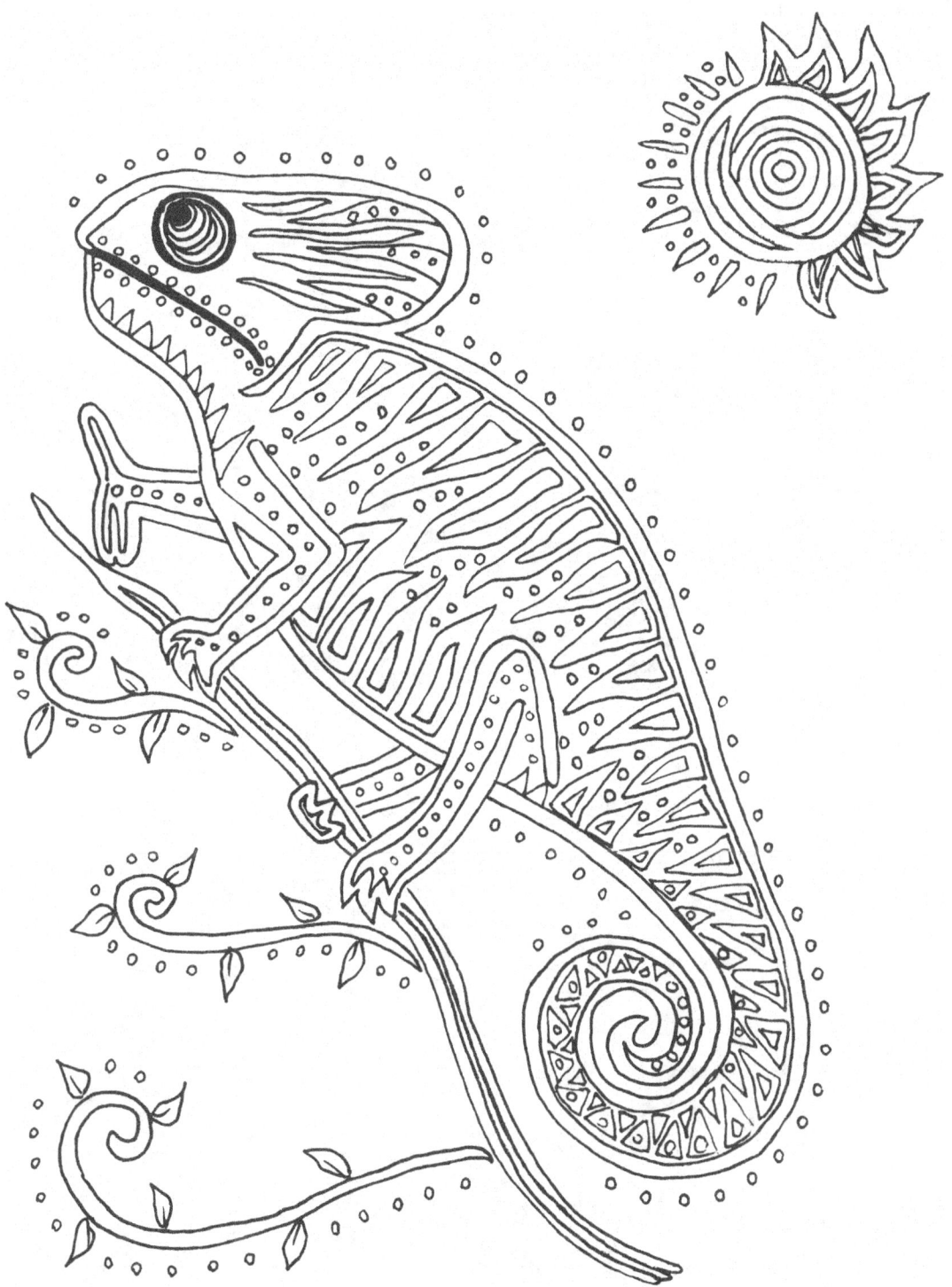

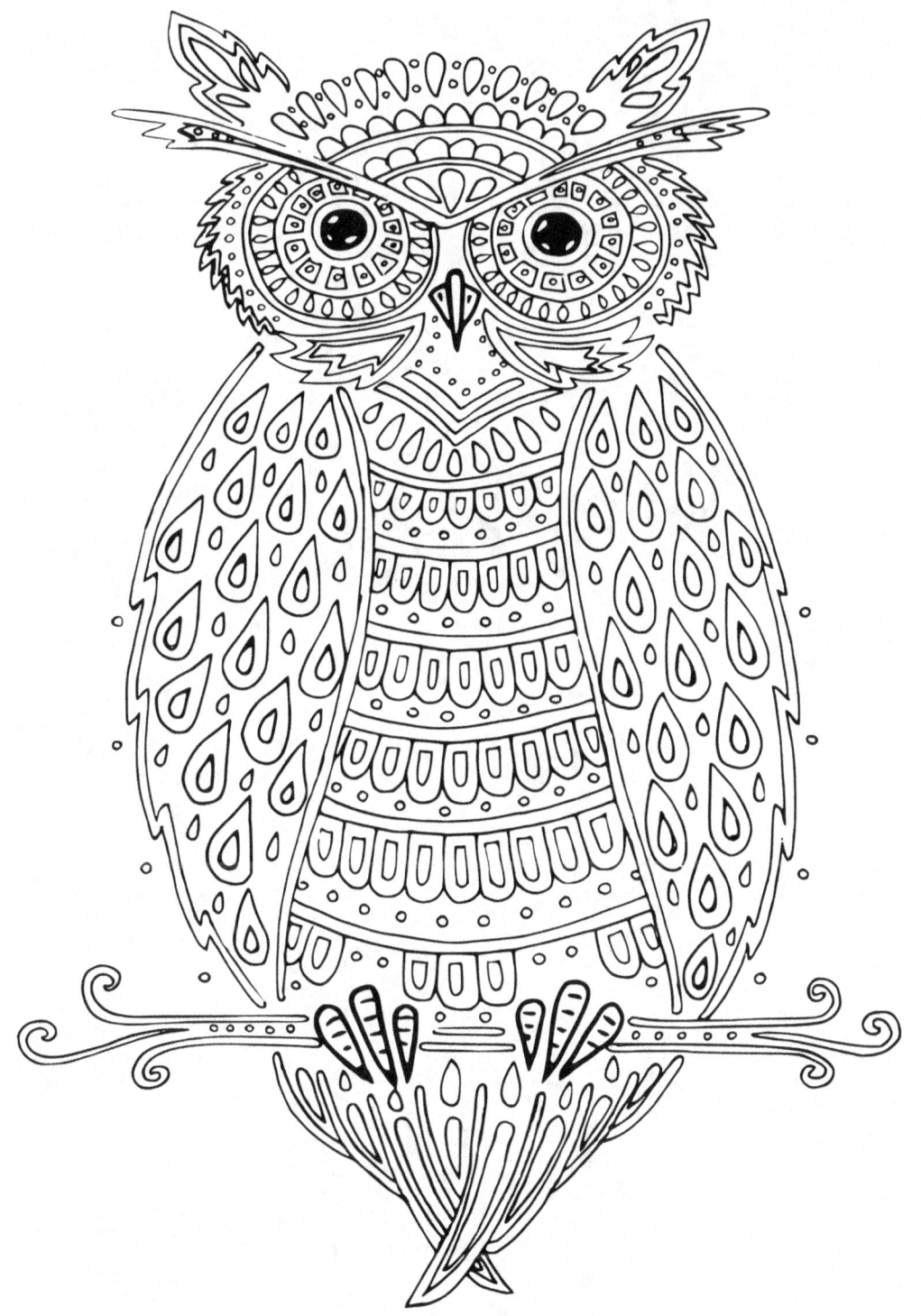

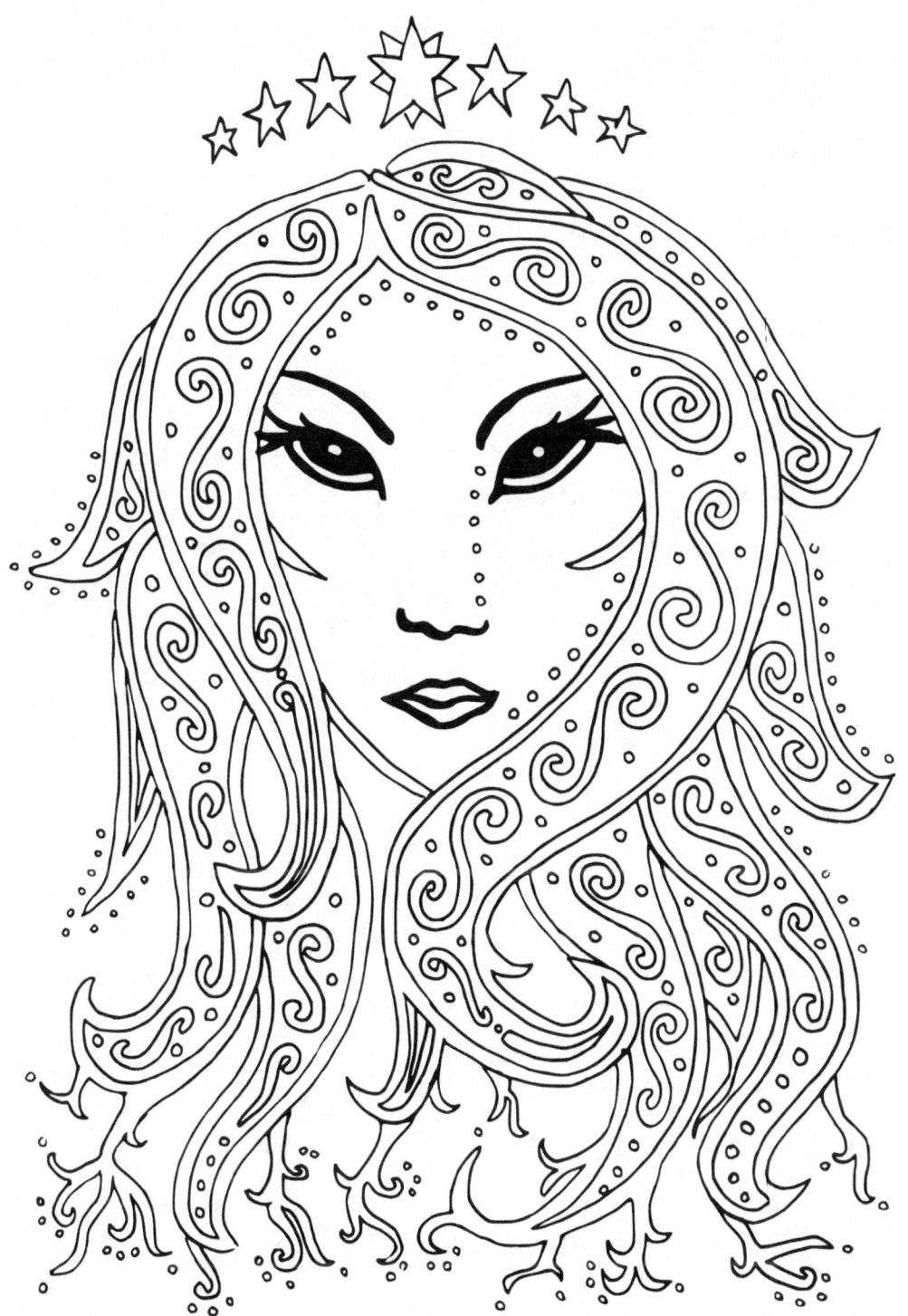

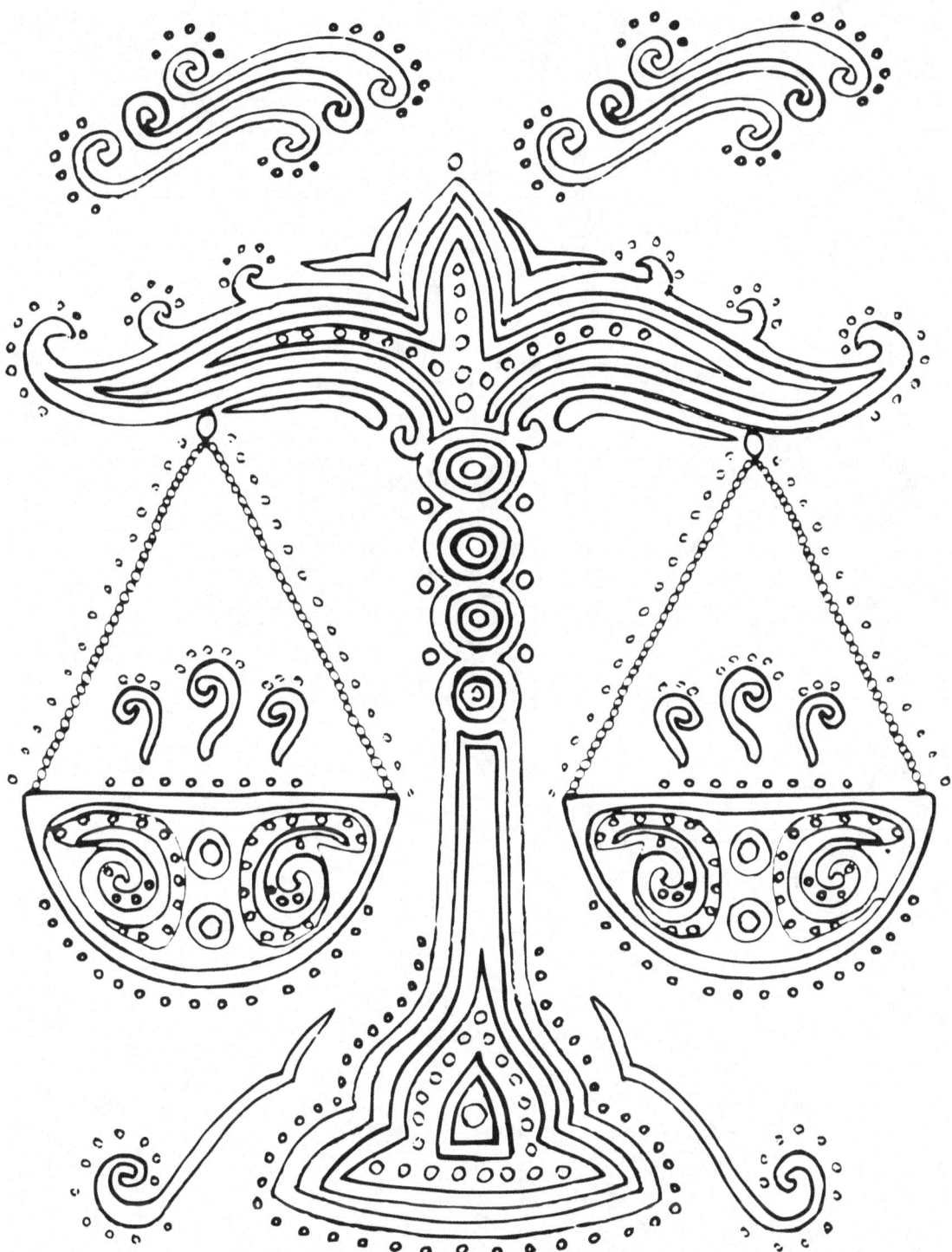

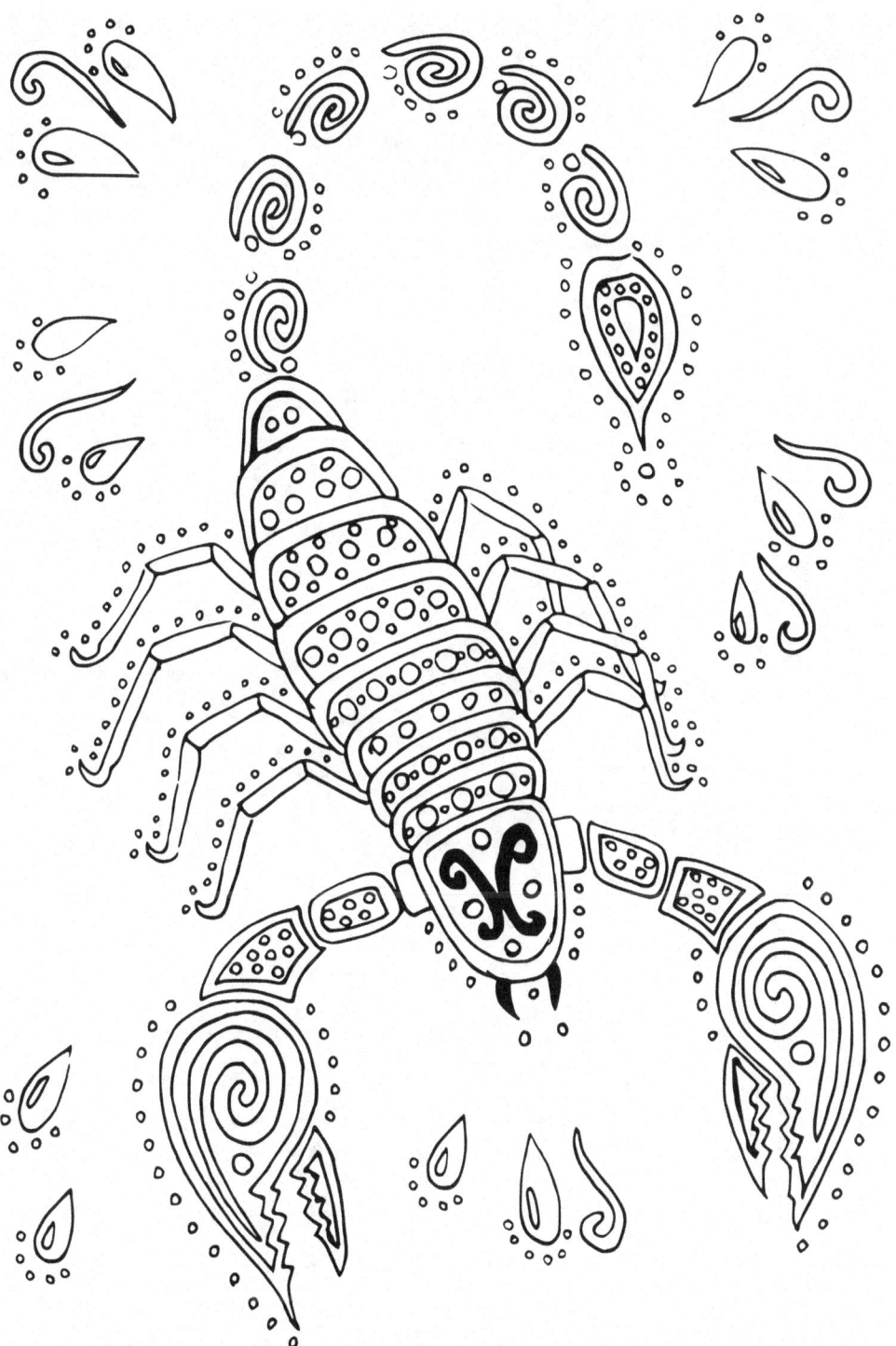

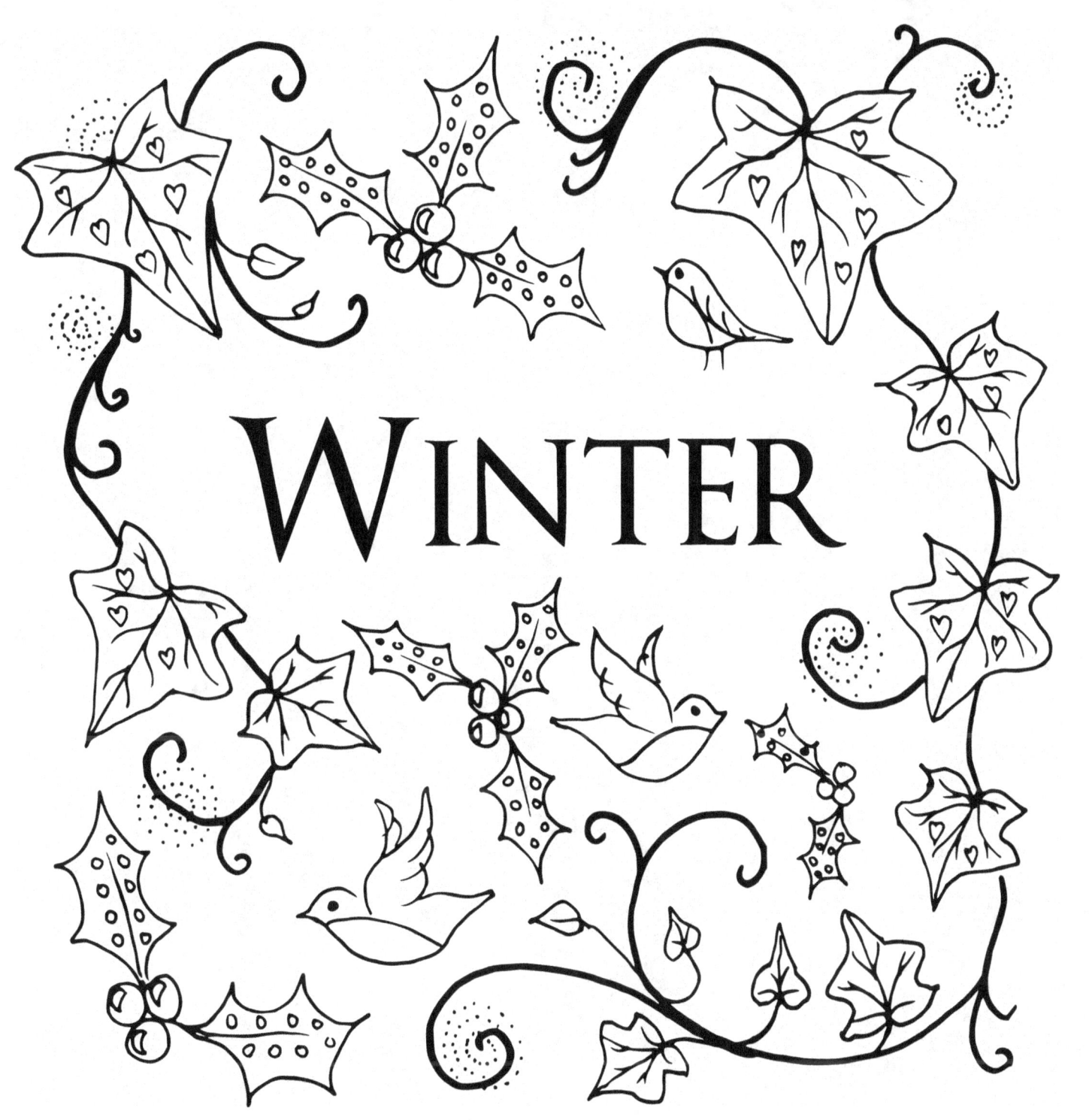

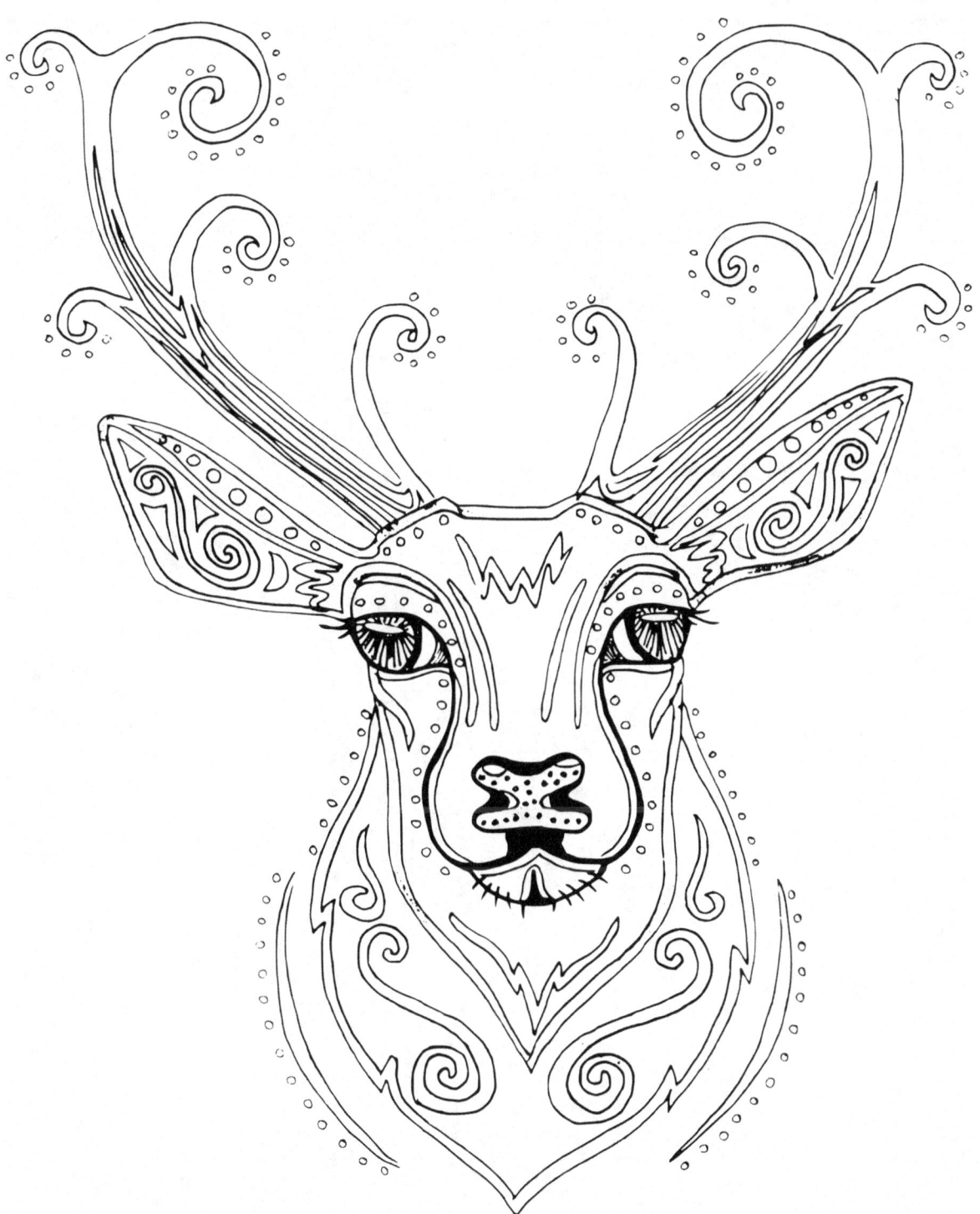

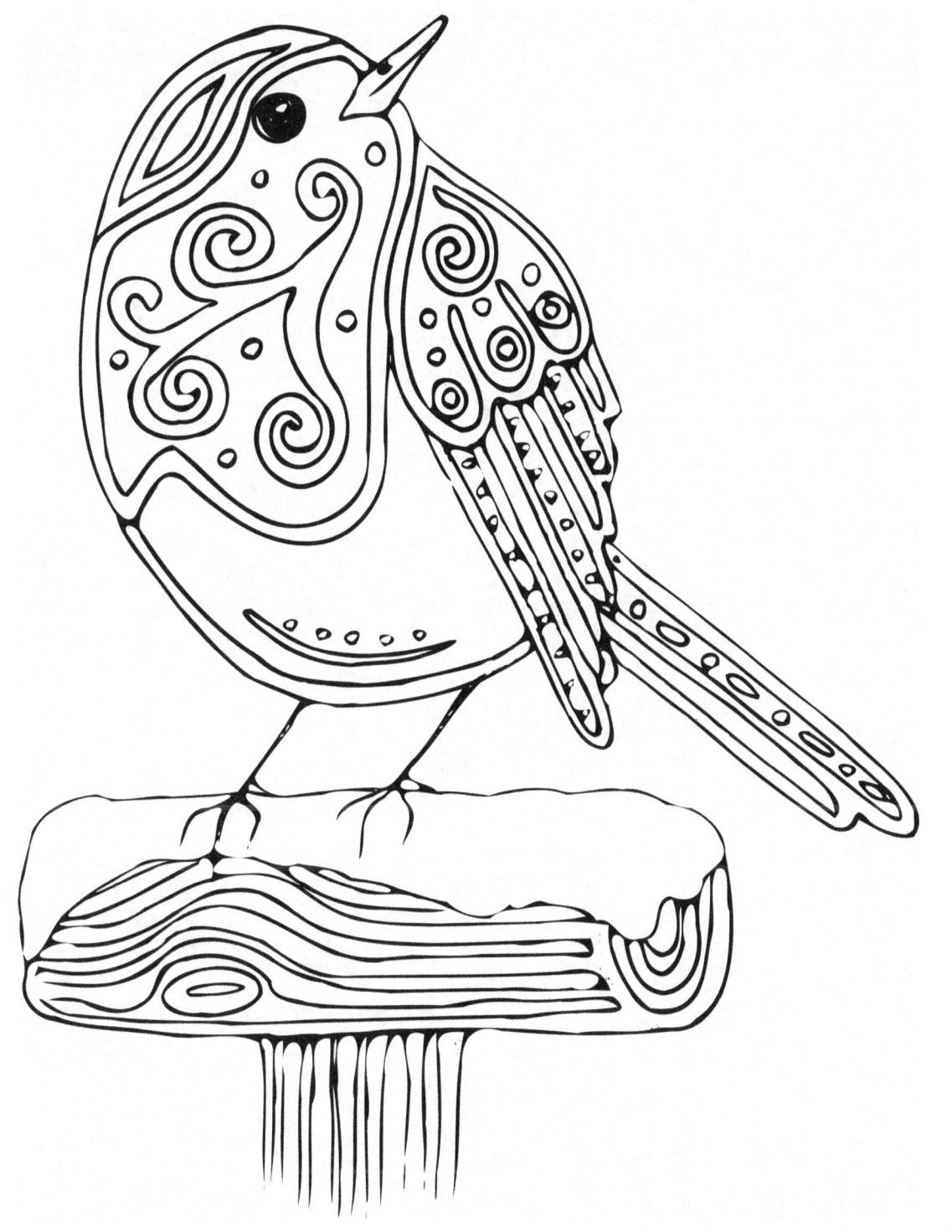

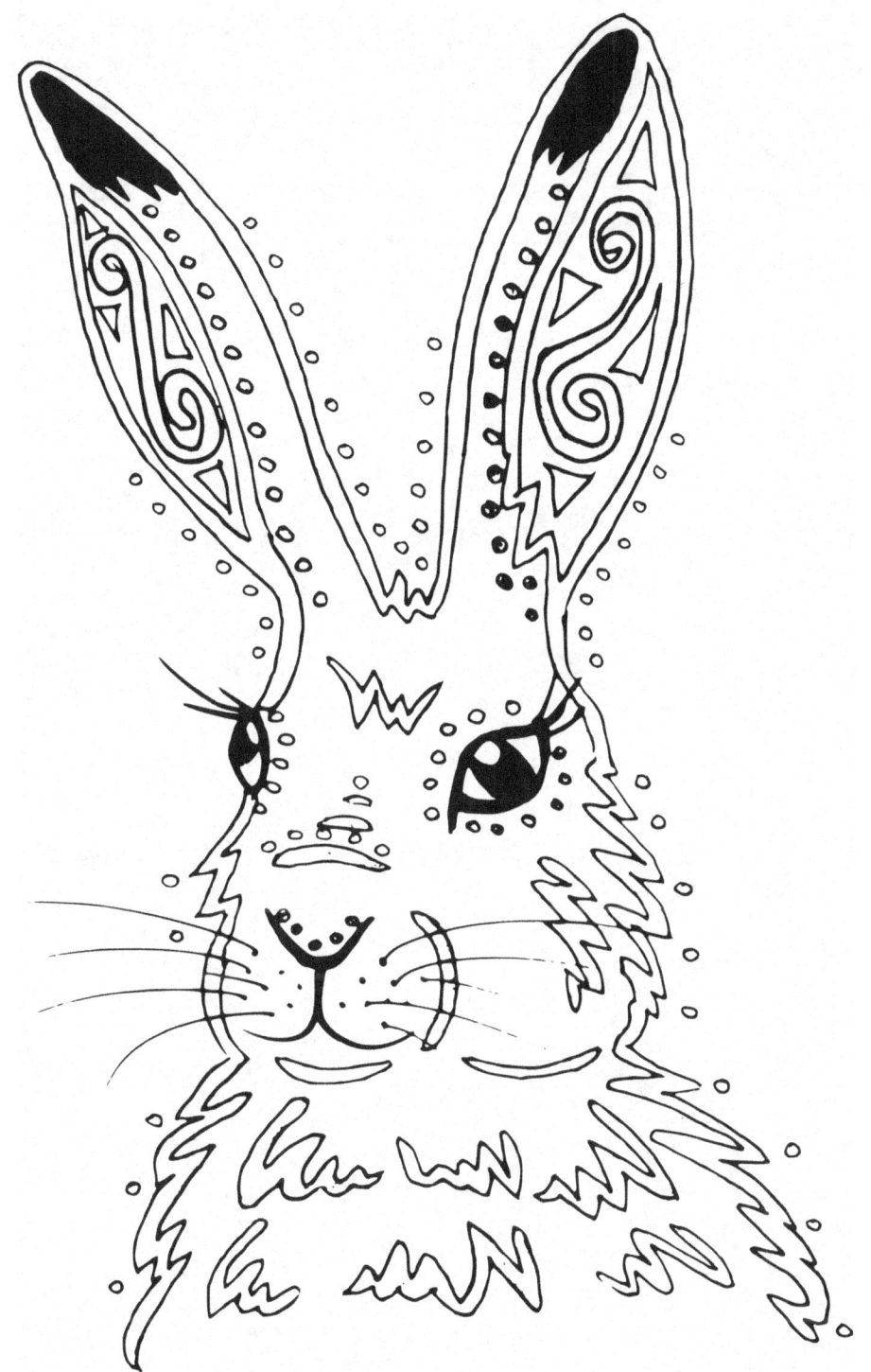

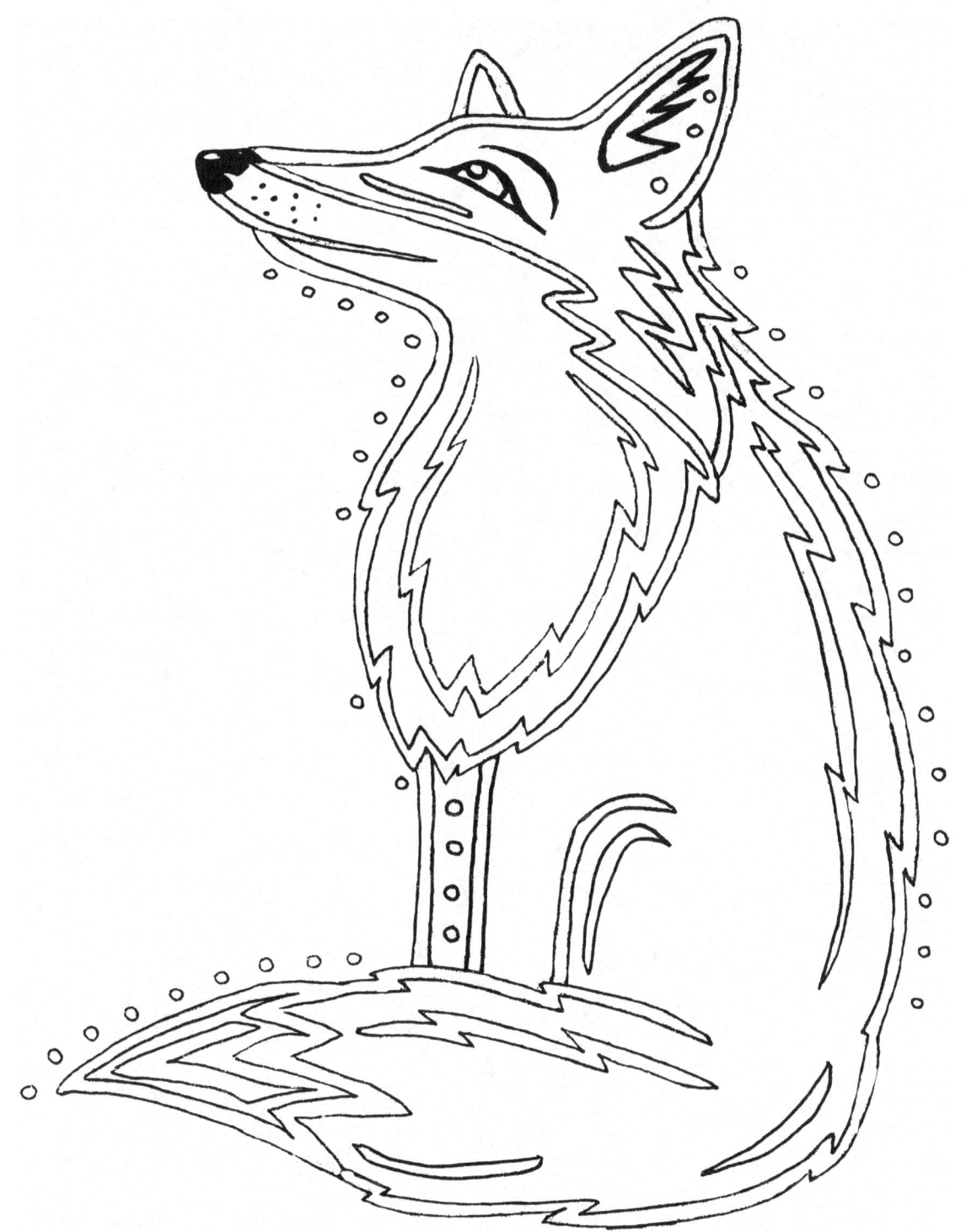

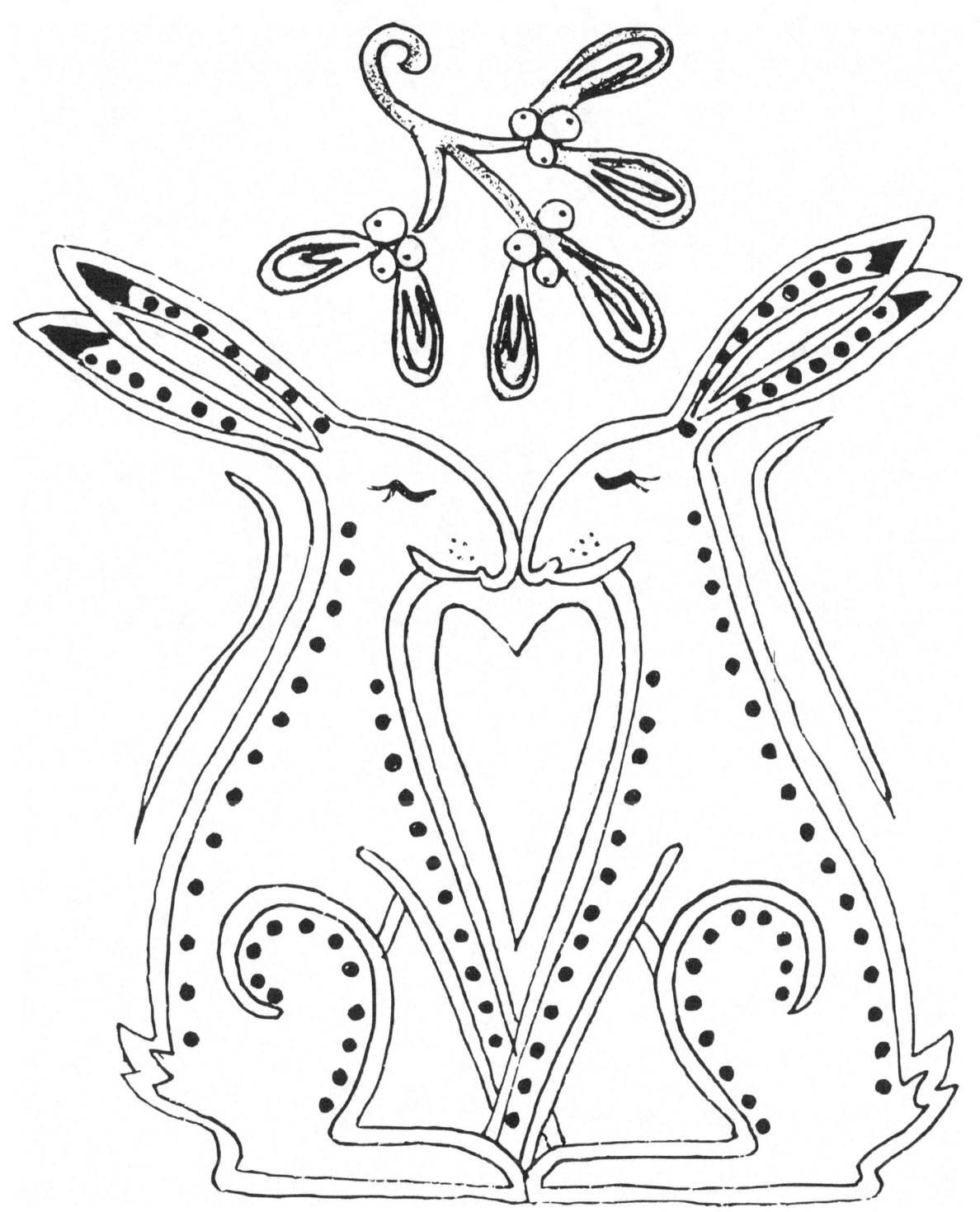

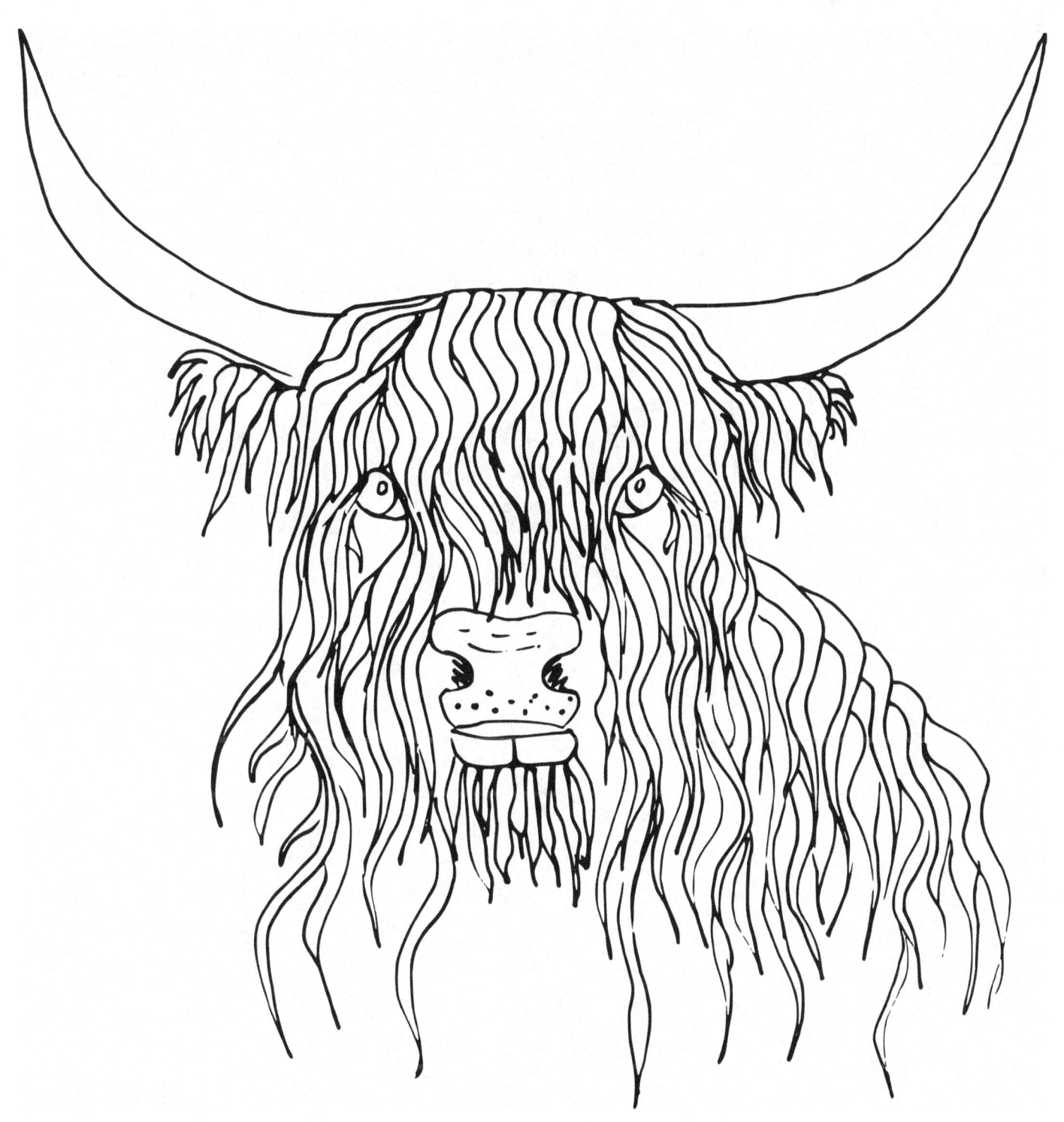

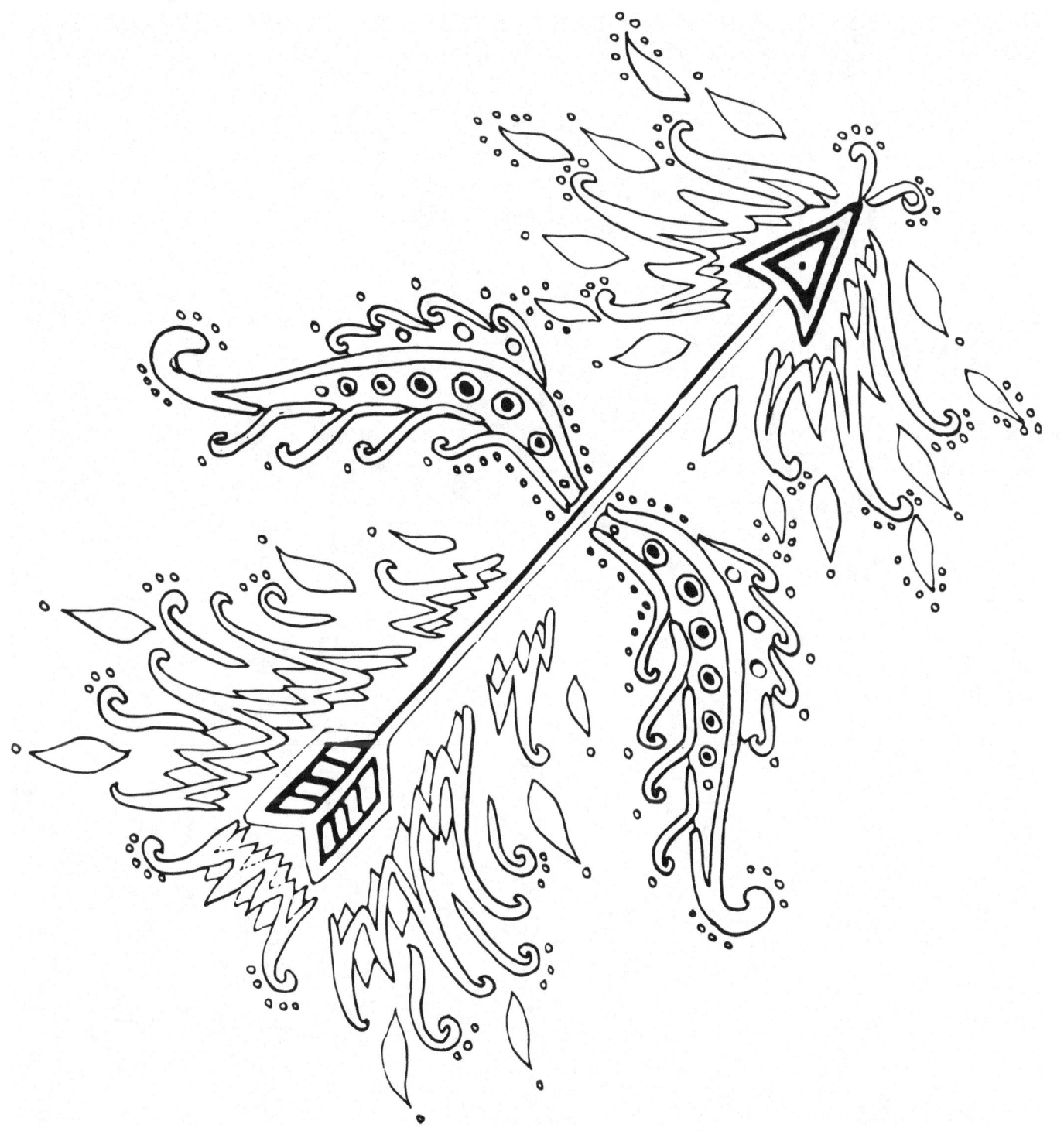

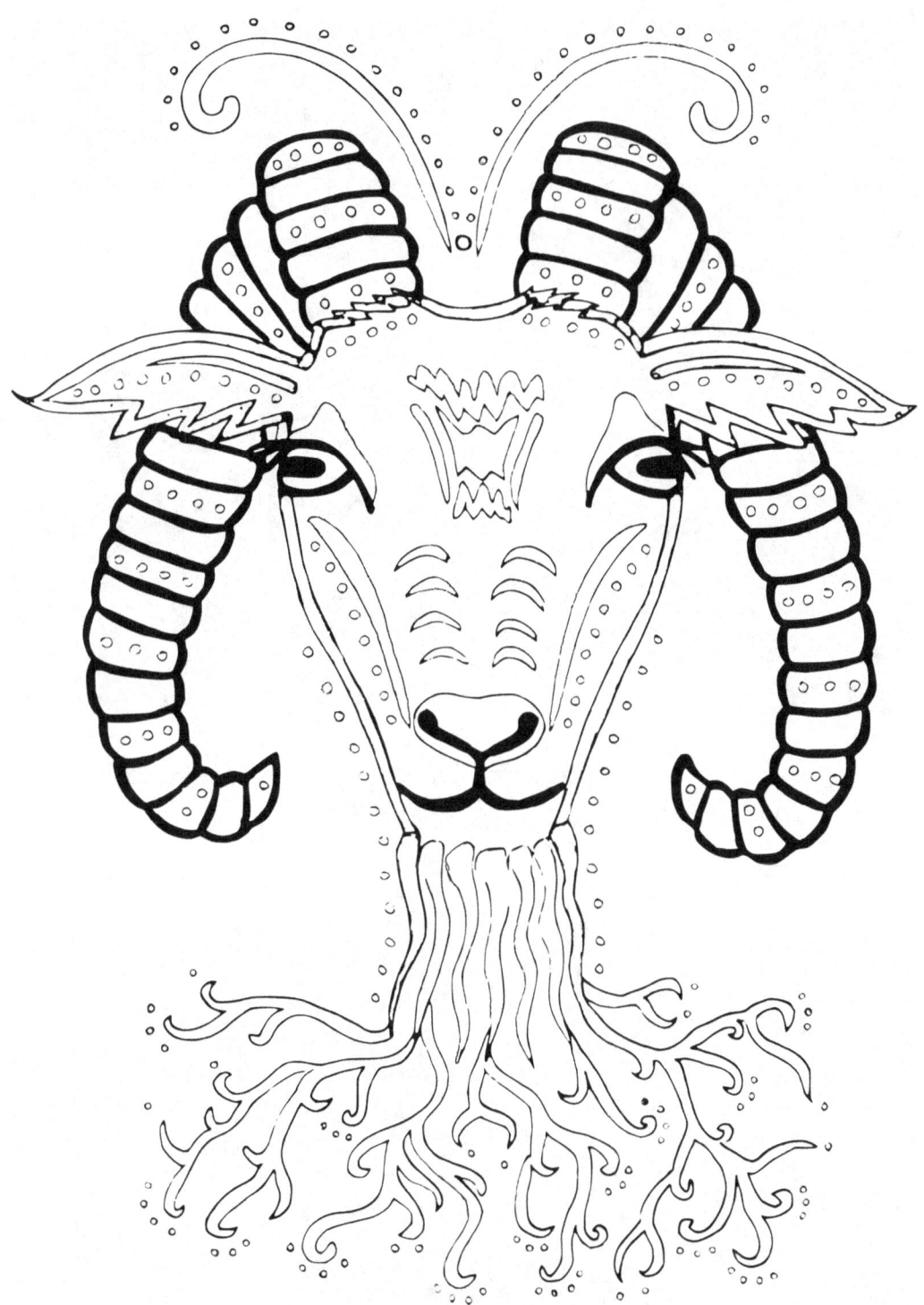

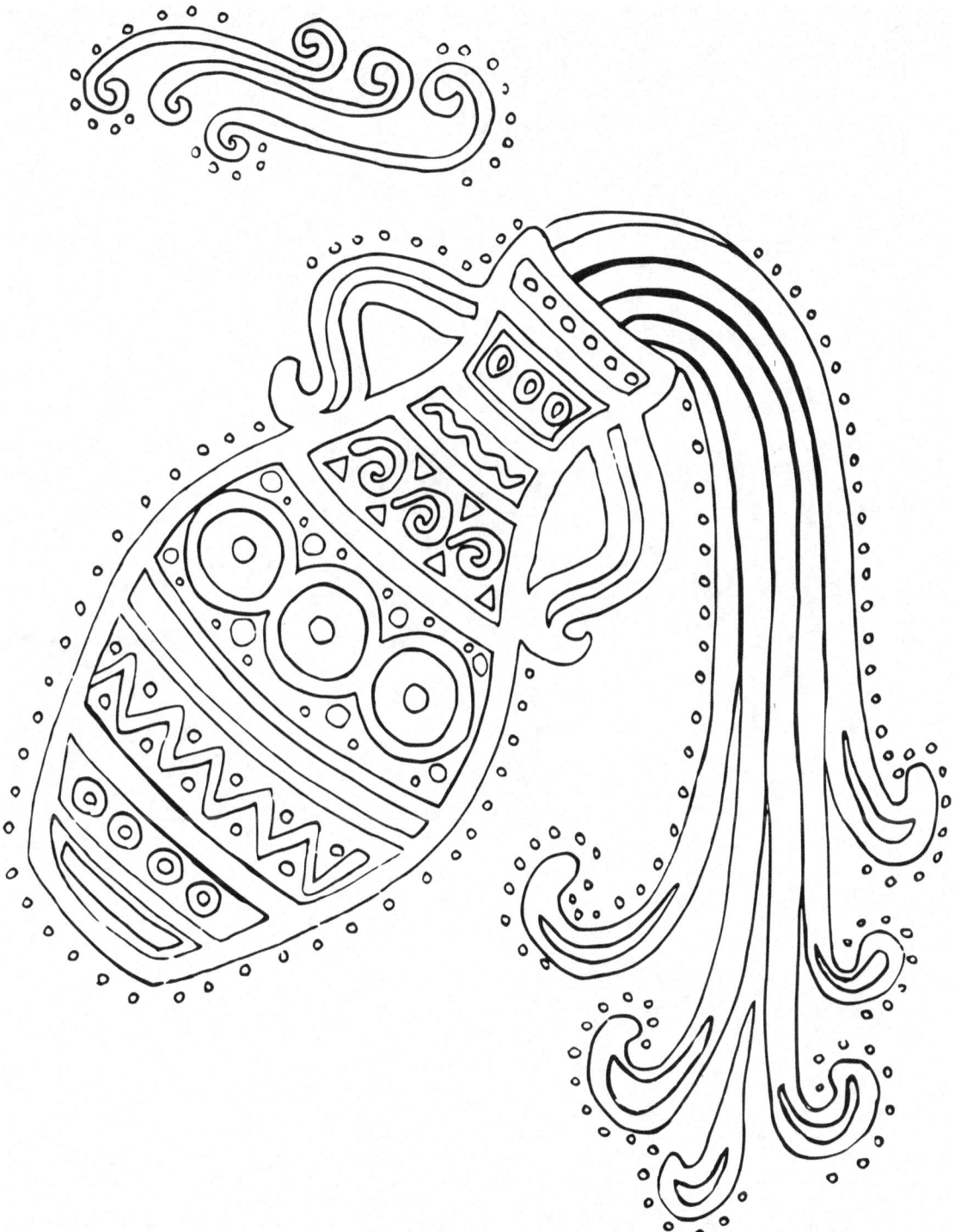

www.ingramcontent.com/pod-product-compliance
Lightning Source LLC
Chambersburg PA
CBHW081607220526
45468CB00010B/2806